THE MASTERY OF OIL PAINTING

Books by Frederic Taubes

The Quickest Way to Paint Well
Better Frames for Your Pictures
The Mastery of Oil Painting

The Technique of Oil Painting
You Don't Know What You Like
Pictorial Composition and the Art of Drawing
The Amateur Painter's Handbook
Anatomy of Genius
Paintings and Essays on Art
Oil Painting for the Beginner
Studio Secrets
The Painter's Question and Answer Book
The Art and Technique of Oil Painting

The Mastery of
OIL
PAINTING

Frederic Taubes

BRAMHALL HOUSE · NEW YORK

ACKNOWLEDGMENTS

I AM especially indebted to Mr. John Walker, Chief Curator of the National Gallery, Washington, D. C., for having contributed special photographs expressly made for this book, and also to the Art Institute of Minneapolis for the details of Rembrandt's "Lucretia." I wish also to acknowledge the contributions of the National Gallery in London, the Boyman's Museum in Rotterdam, and the Central Iconographical Archives for National Art in Brussels. My thanks are also due to the Metropolitan Museum of Art and the Frick Collection.

Invaluable assistance was given me by Mr. Helmut Ruhemann, Consultant Restorer, National Gallery, London; Dr. Paul Coremans, Director, Laboratoire Central des Musées de Belgique, Brussels; Mr. Rutherford J. Gettens, Associate in Research, Freer Art Gallery, Washington, D. C.; and Mr. Sheldon Keck, Restorer, Brooklyn Museum, in reading my manuscript and making important suggestions. My thanks also go to Mr. Donald Pierce, my associate, for helping with many of the experiments described in this book.

This edition published by Bramhall House,
a division of Clarkson N. Potter, Inc.
by arrangement with The Viking Press, Inc.

(E)

1953

Copyright MCMLIII by The Studio Publications, Inc.

LIBRARY OF CONGRESS CATALOG CARD NUMBER 53-7530
Printed in the United States of America

PREFACE

PAINTING and techniques have fascinated me ever since I can remember, but particularly so after becoming acquainted firsthand with the great art treasures of the museums. Back in 1914, I spent many hours at the Imperial Galleries in Vienna, perhaps even longer than the time I spent at school. Probing into the work of the masters became an obsession, and I finally determined on a reconstruction of the processes contained in their great art.

Analyses of master paintings are usually the work of researchers rather than of painters, but it is my contention that while such analyses are helpful, they usually lack the practical information necessary for an artist to attempt any serious reconstruction. I have already written a number of books on esthetics and techniques. In this book emphasis is on the technical discoveries which have occurred during recent years of research and which greatly expand all previous analyses.

I have been helped in the presentation of this material by those people already mentioned in the acknowledgment page. Museums have been very cooperative too in making special photographs which reveal the actual technique of paint application used by certain of the great masters. More important to the reader than anything else I believe is the present approach, which is based on actual experimentation with materials and formulas suggested in written works, plus many new ones discovered by close re-examination of early masterpieces.

CONTENTS

PART TWO

PRESENT-DAY MATERIALS AND TECHNIQUES
FOR MASTER CRAFTSMANSHIP

PART I

How the Old Masters Worked

1

PAINTING GROUNDS AND THE PHYSICAL ASPECT OF THE PAINT SURFACE

General Observations on the Painting Ground

IN OIL OR tempera painting, the choice of a panel or canvas was dictated by technical considerations as well as by certain rigid conventions established by the early schools.

Works done in tempera had to utilize a gesso surface. Intaglios, embossments, gilding, and other such techniques also required the primary application of gesso to a panel. This rigid support was well adapted both to the technique and to such common uses as the wings of an altar. The panel was also a popular choice for any other kind of work where precision and minuteness of execution were required.

While a gesso ground can be the only choice for a tempera painting on a panel, it must be ruled out as a priming for canvas. Not only would it serve no useful purpose from the point of view of technique, but sooner or later such a priming would develop a network of cracks and very likely ruin a painting. The rigidity of a gesso coating is completely unadaptable to the movements—that is to the expansion and contraction—of a hygroscopic fabric.

The preparation of the priming—both gesso for tempera, and white lead, for oil paintings—has remained virtually the same since they first came into general use. That most of the present-day com-

3

mercial canvases are not prepared from white lead is due to expediency or economy rather than improvement of the traditional method.

When we examine the canvas grounds of the old masters, it is obvious that a palette knife was used for spreading the priming onto the surface of the fabric, precisely as we do it today. But, whereas our commercial priming consists, as a rule, of one or at best two layers, it appears that a fabric of rougher texture (used by the old masters) must have received additional coats, for the interstices of their canvases are well clogged with paint. Whenever the grain of these old canvases strikes us as being unduly prominent, it will more likely than not be the effect of improper relining rather than a meager application of paint.

While priming was generally spread on the canvas with a palette knife, it is interesting to observe that only a few early masters used this instrument for actual painting. In the case of paintings with miniaturelike renderings, the reason for this omission is obvious, but even for the larger surfaces the palette knife technique was not generally adopted until much later.

With the exception of the Primitive painters, painting directly on the white canvas ground was not practiced by the old masters. An imprimatura, or an underpainting, preceded the final work. Toned grounds were widely employed and their colors varied—red, brown, gray, pink, yellow.

Physical Aspects of the Paint Surface

Throughout this book, references to the nature of the old masters' paints are numerous; and in the chapter on painting media the problems of their paint diluents are broadly discussed.

From my own practice and from many other indications I have arrived at a conclusion which I would like to state first in brief. If pure linseed oil—or, what is much more likely, stand oil—had been used on surfaces showing glazes that are rich in medium but poor in pigment or on opaque paint passages of "soupy" consistency, in some instances a drip or a slight lowering of the paint film would certainly be apparent today. This condition is nonexistent in all the Flemish paintings I studied and, generally speaking, in all the early paintings where the use of a heavy liquid paint is evident. Hence it is plausible to assume that a resin—specifically a hard resin —must have gone into the composition of the paint used in the manner described above.

We frequently hear that certain very skillful restorers can produce all conceivable effects in any medium; specifically, they can produce

4

effects such as seen, for example, in the work of Rembrandt with tempera or gouache as well as with oil paint. Although this sounds improbable, it is actually true. One of our foremost experts on picture conservation showed me a famous painting by Rembrandt. On a strip added at the bottom of the picture he had painted, in Rembrandt style, with pigments mixed with damar varnish as a sole vehicle. (It should be mentioned that the painting, at one time, had been reduced from its original size). I have to admit that even a close scrutiny of the new canvas did not disclose to me any difference in appearance between the new paint and the old. (The damar-varnish paint was used to make the restored part removable at will.)

In character of paint surface, there is a definite division between paintings up to about the beginning of the sixteenth century and those of the seventeenth and later centuries. Whereas the early paintings remain practically unaffected when cleaned with the most powerful solvents (acetone, for example), later paintings do not show equal resistance, perhaps because of the presence of soft resin in the painting medium.

A curious reference to a supposed use of soft resins by an early master can be found in *The Care of Paintings* (UNESCO, 1951). On the restoration of the "Pietá" by Sebastiano del Piombo (done before 1520) Cesare Brandi writes: "If the weakest known solvent had been employed, in the naive belief that soft resins were not used in the 16th Century, one of the finest masterpieces of the Venetian Renaissance would have been ruined forever." Brandi's finding must be dismissed as erroneous. He published with it an ultraviolet photo which shows that the picture is almost completely covered with retouchings. "So with his [Brandi's] cleaning trial," asserts Helmut Ruhemann, consultant restorer to the National Gallery, London, "he is not likely to have hit on any unretouched spot." Then he adds: "I have cleaned Piombos and Sartos, they are as tough as all the other Renaissance paintings. The old masters were not as ignorant or careless as to paint with soft resins."

The toughness of the linoxyn of the early Flemish paintings is incomparably more pronounced than the toughness of practically all other paintings. It is assumed by experts that a hundred or even two hundred years alone cannot account entirely for this difference in behavior but that a radically different quality of the painting medium is responsible for it. (I am referring here, of course, exclusively to paintings executed in the oil medium and not in tempera.) From the above, one could safely arrive at the conclusion that—if a resin has been used at all—it is a hard resin which is responsible for the impervious quality of these old paint films.

Now, pure stand-oil is an exceedingly durable medium. The ad-

5

dition of a hard resin is not likely to make it more durable, or at least no proof of this is known to exist. My own experiments have shown that a paint film in which a small quantity of hard resin has been incorporated is just as tough as the pure stand oil film—but not tougher. Here, however, I am strongly handicapped by the element of time, since no research data are available and my own paint samples which I have subjected to examination are still too fresh—that is, hardly older than sixteen years.

To continue with these problems, here are a few facts worthy of notice. Not all paintings of the same period behave in the same fashion; some remain in perfect condition for centuries, others deteriorate. Certain paints, even with the same painters, show a marked difference in behavior. For instance, there are paintings by Frans Hals, I am told by one of the best-informed restorers, in which the black is as tough as the rest of the colors. Then again, some of his paintings show an exceedingly fragile black. The same also applies to Rembrandt, where the blacks are often vulnerable; the ochers in these paintings behave in a similar fashion. Now we know that black pigment does not very well solidify when mixed with oil and that ocher, if not freed sufficiently from impurities, can behave capriciously. Moreover, it should be remembered that even the best of pigments may not have been sufficiently dispersed in oil—because of the carelessness of an apprentice, perhaps—and thus may have left a weak paint film in the body of a picture.

Van Dyck's paintings behave unevenly with regard to permanence. The paintings of El Greco and Goya, although two centuries apart, show great toughness. Those of the British school of the eighteenth and especially the nineteenth centuries are often very delicate. On the other hand, some of the French impressionistic paintings (executed with straight linseed oil) evidence toughness comparable to many of the best old masters. It should be noted, however, that many of the impressionistic paintings are in very poor condition because they were painted on an absorbent priming. Such priming will absorb oil from the paint, leaving the pigment without sufficient binder. Or, what is often the case, a quantity of soft resin (mastic or damar) entered the body of the paint, thus making it vulnerable to even a mild organic cleaning agent. Such paintings, frequently because of their weak linoxyn, cannot be restored very well.

Among the British paintings (and there are others), some of the pre-Raphaelites, the Turners, and Whistlers fall within this category. The restorers know well that the cleaning of a Turner (executed in glazes containing mastic) or a Whistler that was painted with a turpentine-diluted oil is a major problem which can be overcome only by extraordinary patience.

It is common knowledge that paint surfaces containing bitumen (which was already in use in the eighteenth century) never solidify in the true sense.

2

EXPERIMENTS WITH TEMPERA AND OIL
TO APPROXIMATE EFFECTS
OF EARLY PAINTINGS

SINCE, in the course of our study, we shall continue to mention tempera painting, certain facts about the medium should be established. There are two general types of tempera: (1) the pure egg tempera which employs the whole of an egg, or the yolk alone, as a binder for the pigments; (2) an artificial emulsion which combines aqueous and oleaginous ingredients in the presence of an emulsifying agent such as gum arabic or egg yolk, for example.

The pure egg-yolk tempera is in the nature of a water color; it will always utilize the white priming of the support and never show any impasto. On the other hand, the oil-water and egg emulsion (with or without an addition of varnish), depending on the quantitative relation of oil and water, can be made to approximate either pure oil or a water-color medium. Hence, if enough oil is used in the formula, it will, from the mere appearance of the paint, be impossible to determine whether we are dealing with a tempera or an oil medium, for a "fat" tempera medium will possess all the outward characteristics of oil paint.

In connection with tempera and oil formulas, the following experiments are interesting. The object of making the test panels illustrated in figures 1 to 4 was to duplicate textural effects found in the paintings of early masters.

7

Figure 1A. The panel for this experiment—and the succeeding ones through figure 4—was primed with gesso, and glazed with resin-oil color. The delineations were made with tube paints thinned with stand oil. The raised effects of the design were achieved, but the manipulation and control were not favorable, and the fineness of the lines is not so pronounced as in figures 2A and 2B.

Figure 1B. On the same ground, tube paints were painted with pure linseed oil as a thinner. This illustrates a complete failure.

Figures 2A (see color section) and *2B.* Over the same ground again, gum tempera was employed for the delineations, made into a wet copal-resin-oil glaze. The gum-tempera formula was mixed as follows:

> 5 parts gum-arabic solution (2 ounces of gum arabic were first dissolved in 5 ounces of water)
> 1 part stand oil
> 1 part Copal Varnish
> (all parts by volume)

The above formula is, of course, not the authentic formula of the old masters; it is one of many possible combinations. The pigments were ground in this medium to a heavy viscous consistency. Such tempera paint, applied to a wet glaze, lends itself to producing the finest and sharpest designs.

Figure 3A demonstrates the use of an egg-tempera emulsion into a wet resin-oil color glaze. This formula, which can be considered more or less standard, was prepared in the following manner:

> 3 parts egg yolk
> 1½ parts water
> 1 part stand oil
> 1 part Copal Varnish

First the oil and the varnish were mixed together and then slowly poured into the egg water, while constantly stirring it with an egg beater. The pigments were ground in this emulsion to a heavy viscous consistency. In my opinion this medium is somewhat less effective than the gum-tempera formula.

Figure 3B. Here about equal parts of tube paint and Copal Concentrate were mixed. The results were good—the best of all the oil and resin-oil media—but the manipulation was not as easy as with the gum-tempera paint. (See color section.)

Figure 4A. The medium used in this example consisted of 1 part of sun-thickened oil, ½ part of Copal Varnish, ½ part of venice

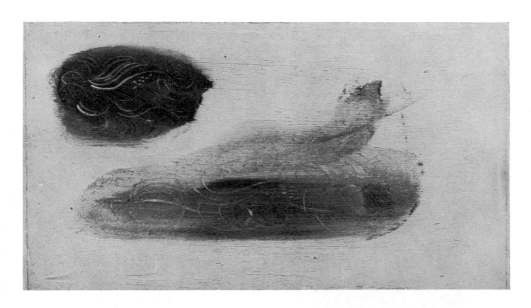

Fig. 1A (upper). Experimental delineations made with pure stand oil medium showing good results and Fig. 1B (lower) with pure linseed oil, showing unsatisfactory results.

Top: Fig. 2B. *Experimental delineations made with* gum *tempera into a wet oil-resin glaze. (See also Fig. 2A in color section.) The textural results clearly resemble effects seen in certain early Renaissance paintings.*
Bottom: Fig. 3A. *Experimental delineations made with* egg *tempera into a wet resin-oil glaze.*

Upper: Fig. 4A. Experimental delineations produced with a medium composed of sun-thickened linseed oil, Copal Varnish, and venice turpentine. Lower: Figure 4B. Experiment using an identical formula except for the use of stand oil in place of sun-thickened oil.

turpentine. The effects produced with this medium were only fair.

Figure 4B. The same experience can be reported here as in the example where pure stand oil was used (figure 1*A*), except that the drying time of the sun-thickened linseed oil was shorter.

3

VAN EYCK
AND EARLY FLEMISH PAINTERS

A GREAT DEAL has been written on the early Flemish painters, and we must explore the statements of the best-known authorities, such as Dr. Paul Coremans, director of the Laboratoire Central des Musées de Belgique, Brussels; Mr. Rutherford J. Gettens, Associate in Research, Freer Art Gallery, Washington, D. C.; M. Jean Thissen, of Dr. Coremans' laboratory; and others. First let us follow the reasoning of A. P. Laurie who, in his last book, *The Technique of the Masters,* discusses the use of stand oil by the Flemish painters. Laurie relates how he requested a sign painter to copy Jan van Eyck's signature from the painting "Marriage of Arnolfini." In using a stand-oil paint for this purpose the sign painter confirmed that this was indeed the material he always employed in his trade; and, by dipping his miniver brush in a black pigment ground in stand oil, he made so faithful a simile of the signature as to satisfy Laurie's conjecture that a miniver brush and stand-oil medium are the substance of the van Eyck method. One can have, indeed, no quarrel with this contention for it is true in lettering that an extra-long sable brush and a viscous paint are the traditional choice. Furthermore, as an experienced user of stand oil for a long time, I can say that there has never been any doubt in my mind about the presence of

12

stand-oil paints in most of the fifteenth-century panels. By experimentation and study this fact becomes obvious.

However, Laurie makes no reference to the possibility of a resin content in the paint; and we know definitely that, besides oil, another substance is present in the van Eyck medium and this substance can be only a hard resin. An analysis of van Eyck's paintings a little farther on in this chapter gives us further evidence to support this fact.

Meanwhile, refer to the test panels shown in figure 1*A* and 4*B*. The line formations and textures produced with a stand-oil-prepared paint and a proper brush must be considered more or less identical with those observed in early Flemish (as well as certain German and Italian) paintings. It seems to me also that the paint used for this purpose should be not merely tempered with a thermally processed oil but that some of the pigments should be ground in it. Here the proper density (pigment saturation) of the semiliquid paint is of prime importance. Paint sufficiently thick will stay on the canvas without sliding down; but, as mentioned earlier, when "soupiness" occurs, a "drip" will usually result. It is reasonable to assume that, in the preparation of a thick and at the same time limpid paint, a 100 per cent assurance of obtaining a "nondrip" material is improbable, but a small addition of a hard resin will give us precisely such an assurance.

The possibility that tempera paint in combination with oil was used in many of the early Flemish works showing miniaturelike execution of details is also to be seriously considered, as demonstrated in figures 2*A* and *B*.

I do not remember precisely where the suggestion of painting with a tempera medium on the wet oil paint first appeared in print, but this technique is certainly capable of producing the effects which are so characteristic of some of the Flemish, German, and early Renaissance paintings. In the fifteenth century, tempera and, separately, oil media were employed in different parts of the same painting.

In any discussion of the Flemish school we must find ourselves inevitably returning to Jan van Eyck. As Max J. Friedlander says: ". . . He is supposed to have invented 'oil painting.' There is a hard core of truth to this traditional legend. But Jan van Eyck did not paint as he did because he had invented something; rather he invented or discovered a certain pictorial technique because he was unable to reproduce his visional experience with the technique he had inherited."

Although I had studied Flemish works both here and abroad, I felt that no chapter on this subject could be written without consultation with Dr. Coremans in Brussels. Hence in the spring of 1952

I visited the Laboratoire Central des Musées de Belgique in Brussels and was privileged to look at the latest data of research done by Dr. Coremans and his staff on the occasion of the restoration of the Ghent altar. Examinations of this work can further assist us in piecing together the van Eyck technique.

Since the method of Jan van Eyck (c.1380-1441) is justly looked upon as a break with earlier traditions, certain authors try to explain the change in the light of purely esthetic considerations, and some technicians believe that it is the nature of the binder that is responsible for the different approach in painting. Historical sources reveal that the drying oil (we may as well say linseed oil, since the specific origin of the oil is not determinable) was known and used long before van Eyck. Now, at last, the physical and chemical examination of the binder, as well as microscopic studies of cross cuts of paint samples taken from van Eyck's work, allow us to make well-founded conclusions. These conclusions definitely discount the one-time assumption of a combined tempera-oil technique and make us accept the presence of a siccative oil as a basic substance of the binder.

According to Dr. Coremans, there is no doubt that van Eyck's oil medium contained a substance showing characteristics of natural resins. However, the quantity of the substance varied. In the glazed parts of his painting, the "Adoration of the Lamb" in the Church of St. Bavon, Ghent, the ingredient appeared to be considerably increased in quantity. It is also evident in this painting that tempera was not used. By experimentation we can readily discover that dried oil, with or without the admixture of resin, regardless of its age, breaks up into tiny globules of fat under action of hydrochloric acid, whereas tempera remains impervious to alkali and strong acids. A test was carried out on the paint specimens taken from the van Eyck panels, which proved this point.

Another interesting fact that helps to prove van Eyck's use of hard resin (besides a reference by Theophilius and the importation of such resins into Europe from overseas at the time) is the discovery that turpentine was used at a much earlier date than hitherto believed. (As we know, turpentine is the important solvent for resin varnishes.) Laurie puts the introduction of turpentine at the end of the fifteenth or the start of the sixteenth centuries. However, documents in the archives of Bruges seem to invalidate this theory. Already in 1345-1346 (hence long before van Eyck) we find the term "alembic," "turpentine," and "brandy" (Coremans). With the existence of an alembic, the "modern" distillation method becomes feasible, and the employment of resin in volatile, as well as in oleaginous, solutions is probable.

14

The ground on which this famous painting was done was pre-pared with gesso (applied, of course, to a panel). In the strictest sense, however, we should not refer to gesso in connection with Flemish painting, for gesso signifies the use of calcium sulphate (found on the panels of the Italian Primitives), whereas calcium car-bonate—that is, a chalk ground—was used by the Northern School.

Although we have hitherto supposed that a glue size was used for the isolation of any (size-bound) ground, this has not been substan-tiated by the chemical analysis of particles taken from the van Eyck panels. Hence the assumption that a resin served to make the ground non-absorbent is more than likely. Actual painting was done on top of the white panels without the use of an imprimatura, and a micro-scopic examination of a paint particle cross section reveals that in this instance we are dealing with a number of superimposed layers of paint, a method entirely different from that found in earlier or contemporary paintings of his day. Here the masterly exploitation of the qualities of transparency and opacity of paint, together with the use of an appropriate medium, gives the colors a hitherto un-known brilliance and depth, and the appearance of enamel.

Although van Eyck's painting is executed in pure oil color, there is one exception when the use of tempera appears and that is when lapis lazuli and at times azurite blue were employed. This is not surprising if we consider that the blue pigments mentioned will turn much darker in tone when compounded with linseed oil. The cir-cumstance that a layer of such a tempera color was found on top of an oil-paint stratum does not make it illogical if we assume that an intermediate film of varnish (on top of the oil paint, and before the subsequent tempera application) was the factor that allowed such a combination.

A sample of paint (together with the ground and the layers of old varnish on top of the paint) which I had the opportunity of examin-ing under a microscope in Dr. Coremans' laboratories consisted of four independent layers of paint—opaque layers, scumbles, and a glaze—which were superimposed to produce definite effects. In cer-tain parts of the panel more than four layers of paint were found. My original assumption that the high impasti effects observed in the details from the polyptych (see my experiment, figures 2*A* and 2*B*) were perhaps carried out in gum tempera was not shared by Dr. Coremans. Specific reference is made here to the van Eyck panels examined by Dr. Coremans and not to the Primitives in general.

Backed by results of an unassailable scientific examination, we are

15

Fig. 5. *Jan van Eyck (1370?–1440). "Adoration of the Lamb" (detail).*

Above and left: Figs. 5A, 5B. Other details from Jan van Eyck's "Adoration of the Lamb."

*Figs. 5C (opposite page),
5D (above) and 5E (left).
More details from Jan
van Eyck's "Adoration of
the Lamb."*

19

thus obliged to accept oil and a hard resin as the only medium employed by van Eyck. As an acceptable proof that resin did enter into some oil layers, I repeat the discovery that the substance showing resinous characteristics was present in increased quantity in the glazes. In the composition of the glazes, as we know, the resin would play an important role.

As a curious finding, it can be related that parts of the original painting by van Eyck, such as the inscription and the Crown (see figure 5D), are not original but later additions. These additions are painted on top of a silver foil which was placed on the surface (by means of a mordant) to cover up the original paint. On the grounds of existing evidence it can be said that these (as well as some other overpaints) were carried out by Jan van Scorel and Lancelot Blondeel in 1550. The interesting circumstance here is that the van Eyck workshop traditions at the time of these additions or overpaints —that is, about 120 years after the completion of the altar piece— remained essentially unchanged, for there is no difference at all in the appearance of these and the older paint-surface characteristics.

4

ANALYSIS OF SELECTED FIFTEENTH- AND SIXTEENTH-CENTURY PAINTINGS

BEFORE ANALYZING in some detail specific paintings of different schools by notable masters who lived near the time of van Eyck, I would like to refer once more to the experiments shown in figures 2*A* and *B* in relation to the work of Bartolommeo Vivarini (1432-? 1491) and Lucas van Leyden (1494-1533), who are singled out as quite typical practitioners of a certain very detailed technique followed out in medieval Italy and the Low Countries. When gum tempera colors are painted on the wet oil glaze, hard, sharp, miniaturelike effects can be produced such as in the Vivarini (Italian) panel, figure 6, and the van Leyden (Dutch) panel, figure 7. Although no one short of an eye witness in the workshop of these masters could claim that this actually was the technique used in these works, certainly the paint construction very closely resembles it in appearance. Other paintings with small and elaborate detail work by both Flemish and Italian masters of about this time could be chosen for similar comparison.

From Vivarini and Lucas van Leyden, we turn to a very puzzling example by Cornelis Matsys (c.1508-?1580), an artist who lived in approximately the same period. Not only is this example equally remote from our conception of oil painting but also thoroughly mystifying in its technical aspect.

21

Cornelis Matsys (c.1508-?1580). Flemish. "Imaginary Landscape"
(Detail), Figure 8

A greater contrast in conception and procedure between that of the "Primitives" and the "modern" school of Titian, for example, can hardly be imagined. In this case we cannot even refer to "painting" in the usual sense, but to "coloring," perhaps, to use Rembrandt's own word in connection with such a technique. Here, over a perfectly worked-out, completely delineated drawing, with all the details in definite arrangement, the final colors were applied. Furthermore, the coloring started from an entirely arbitrary point. For example, we perceive, not without wonderment, that even the *staffages,* the tiny figures, were put in at this initial stage, all finished, with the high light well in strategic position.

Why the painter chose to paint the heavy green masses first (apparently in an oil medium on a multicolored imprimatura which covers the entire panel) is also difficult to understand. It is obvious that painting of the spaces around the contours of the trees must have presented a major difficulty and involved very tedious work, to say the least.

It would seem that, had Matsys planned to work in tempera first, the parts to be finished in oil should have been painted last. This, however, is not the case in our panel. Hence the condition of the picture at the initial stage seems totally incongruous to me.

From present-day understanding of techniques, it is equally difficult to comprehend how a painter could proceed in piecing such disjointed details together without losing sight of the whole, or how any balance or pictorial coherence could be maintained. The painting which seems to combine so many irreconcilable beginnings is introduced into this study as an interesting example of a needlessly difficult technique for which no ready explanation can be given.

Jan Gossaert [Mabuse] (1478?-?1533). Flemish. "Adoration of the Magi," Figure 9

This painting is executed in the typical manner of Flemish oil painting. Deviating hardly at all from the precepts of the van Eycks, it is a truly breathtaking Gothic conception. In spite of the miniaturelike character of the details and the clutter of minutiae, the large and daring design does not suffer at all. This is so because all details are completely subordinated to the composition as a whole, and in the total ornamentation they deliver just the right note.

Giovanni di Paolo (1403-1483). Sienese. "Adoration of the Magi"
(Detail), Figure 10

Luca Signorelli (1441-1523). Umbrian. "Eunostos of Tanagra" (Detail), Figure 11

These two paintings are included as typical examples of tempera technique. If we disregard the "quaintness" of perspective in such paintings and the fascination which the archaic holds for us, the dot-for-dot and hatched-line technique is indeed of little interest either as craftmanship or as personal expression. While di Paolo's painting is pure egg tempera, the Signorelli reveals partial overpainting in oil over the egg-tempera base. Although neither is a particularly early example, it is interesting to note the archaic style employed, which is a result of the tempera medium itself. As always, the technique confines the painter to rather narrow limits of expression.

The pure egg-tempera medium, although it lends itself to the execution of minute details, does not produce the articulate acuteness and plasticity of tempera-in-oil or the pure oil of the Flemish or later Italian Renaissance masters.

Domenico Ghirlandaio (1449-1494). Florentine. "A Lady of the Sassetti Family" (Detail), Figure 12

The rigid routine of the medieval tempera painter prevails here with authority. The modeling is achieved by hatching in pure egg-tempera colors, and the white of the support provides the "inner light." The background is raised in strong relief, which implies that the paint level of the head on the panel is lower than that of the background. The latter, in keeping with certain traditions of the tempera painters, is carried out in a heavy, heat-processed oil paint.

The reason for what seems to us like an incompatible alliance is a technical rather than an esthetic one. A dark, deep tone possessing a velvety depth cannot well be produced in a tempera medium. On the other hand, the heavy oil paint is wonderfully adapted to give a sumptuous cameo appearance to the contours of a figure, as well as richness to foliage or draperies. This seems to be one explanation why many works from the "tempera age" show applications of oil paint in parts. Of course, varnish (especially an oil varnish) lends depth to any flat tone and thus simulates the effect of oil paint. And varnishing of tempera paintings was a common practice in medieval times.

In the background of this painting, an appreciable thickness of the paint layer is apparent. This can best be produced in straight oil medium and also in an oil-tempera emulsion. It should be noted, however that an emulsion rich in oil is much more kindred to the pure oil than to the pure egg medium and, for all practical purposes, it is indistinguishable from the former.

According to Ruhemann, the raised dark areas in tempera (and Primitive oil painting) can also be explained by the fact that some of the dark colors require much medium, and a thick application is needed to produce a dark effect on a white ground. The blues and greens are more raised than the flesh colors because they are under-painted with thick lighter blues and greens.

Carlo Crivelli (active 1457-c.1495). Italian. "Annunciation," Figure 13

In this Renaissance panel, Gothic painting finds its most eloquent expression. Here the lavish gold applications are not merely incidental adornments. Like the paint itself, the gold takes on the function of a color. In fact, the gold was painted on, as can be seen from the brush strokes in the detail (figure 13A); all the light lines and light accents on the wing, the feather, and the ornaments were done in gold. The manner of producing such effects is very simple.

On the finished, dry painting, the surfaces to be gilded were painted over with a small sable brush dipped in a mordant which is prepared from a quick-drying oil varnish. Today, however, we would simply use a commercial gold size which is perfectly adequate for such a purpose. From here on the process and the materials are the same. When the mordant or size is tacky, the gold leaf is placed over the entire area that has been treated. Then when the mordant is completely dry (and this—depending on its nature—may take a few hours or perhaps up to twenty-four hours), the gold is rubbed off with the finger. It can be quickly removed from all surfaces not directly treated with the mordant, but it will firmly adhere to the brush strokes established in the mordant. Thus the brush strokes will retain their characteristic appearance.

Gold applied by means of an oil mordant does not lend itself very well to burnishing. When a highly burnished gold effect is seen on medieval tempera paintings, this means that an aqueous mordant was used—one prepared from gum arabic, gelatine, or the white of egg. (The white of egg preparation is generally referred to as glair; it served chiefly for use in gold applications on illuminated manuscripts). Of course, powdered gold can also be dispersed in an aqueous gum arabic solution, and used in the manner of water color.

24

Michelangelo (1475-1564). Italian. "Madonna, Child, Saint John, and Angels," Figure 14

Apart from the masterly composition and draftsmanship, this unfinished work attributed to Michelangelo is of especial interest to us in that—unlike most of the Renaissance paintings—the flesh tone received an underpainting in a uniformly colored middle tone, approximating the color of terre-verte. Upon the cool green, a warm darker flesh tone was painted on thinly in oil and heightened in the areas of the light, thus producing a subtle modeling in two tones, giving the figures the appearance of statues. Since terre-verte, because of its lack of opacity and faint tinting power, is unsuitable for use in oil painting, it is logical to assume that the pigment must have been ground in a tempera medium.

In Cennino Cennini's *Handbook* we find a reference to the use of terre-verte for underpainting flesh but no mention is made of the vehicle. This has led to the illogical habit of the manufacturers of putting out this color as an oil paint. However, in the Michelangelo painting the green color could have been just as well an oil-paint mixture approximating the color of terre-verte.

Lorenzo di Credi (1459-1537). Italian. "Portrait of a Lady," Figure 15

On the otherwise smooth surface of the picture, the tall trees are painted in high relief of threadlike thickness. The frequent recurrence of such effects in sixteenth-century paintings cannot be looked upon as anything other than a firmly established workshop tradition.

Other examples of such contrasts in technique on a single canvas are given in this book and in more characteristic form, but here the particular beauty of the delicate foliage lacework is worthy of special note. Another point of special interest in Credi's painting is the appearance of the hands. There is irrefutable evidence here that an underpainting in neutral tones—quite customary with the cinquecento painters—preceded the painting of the flesh in color. In contrast to the face, which retained the natural coloring, the hands appear executed in grisaille. Now this might seem like an isolated incident, but it is not. In a scrutiny of other early portrait paintings in museums, this contrast—gray hands and flesh-colored head—can be found in a number of other examples, especially of the Netherland and German schools. The explanation may be quite simple. As every painter who works in grisaille knows, when he has finished a head to his satisfaction—and, more than that, to the satisfaction of the sitter—his interest in the work can very often slump. Not neces-

Fig. 6. Bartolommeo Vivarini (1432–?1491). "Adoration of the Magi" (detail).

Top: Fig. 7. Lucas van Leyden (1494–1533). "Adoration of
the Magi" (detail). Bottom: Fig. 8. Cornelius Matsys (1508?–
?1580). "Imaginary Landscape" (detail).

Fig. 9. Jan Gossaert [Mabuse] (1478?-?1533). "Adoration of the Magi"

Fig. 10. Giovanni di Paolo (c. 1403–1482). "The Adoration of the Magi." Below: Fig. 10A. Detail from the same picture.

(Kress Collection) (National Gallery of Art, Washington)

Fig. 11. Luca Signorelli (1441–1523). "Eunostos of Tanagra" (detail).

Fig. 12. Domenico Ghirlandaio (1449–1498). "A Lady of the Sasetti Family" (detail).

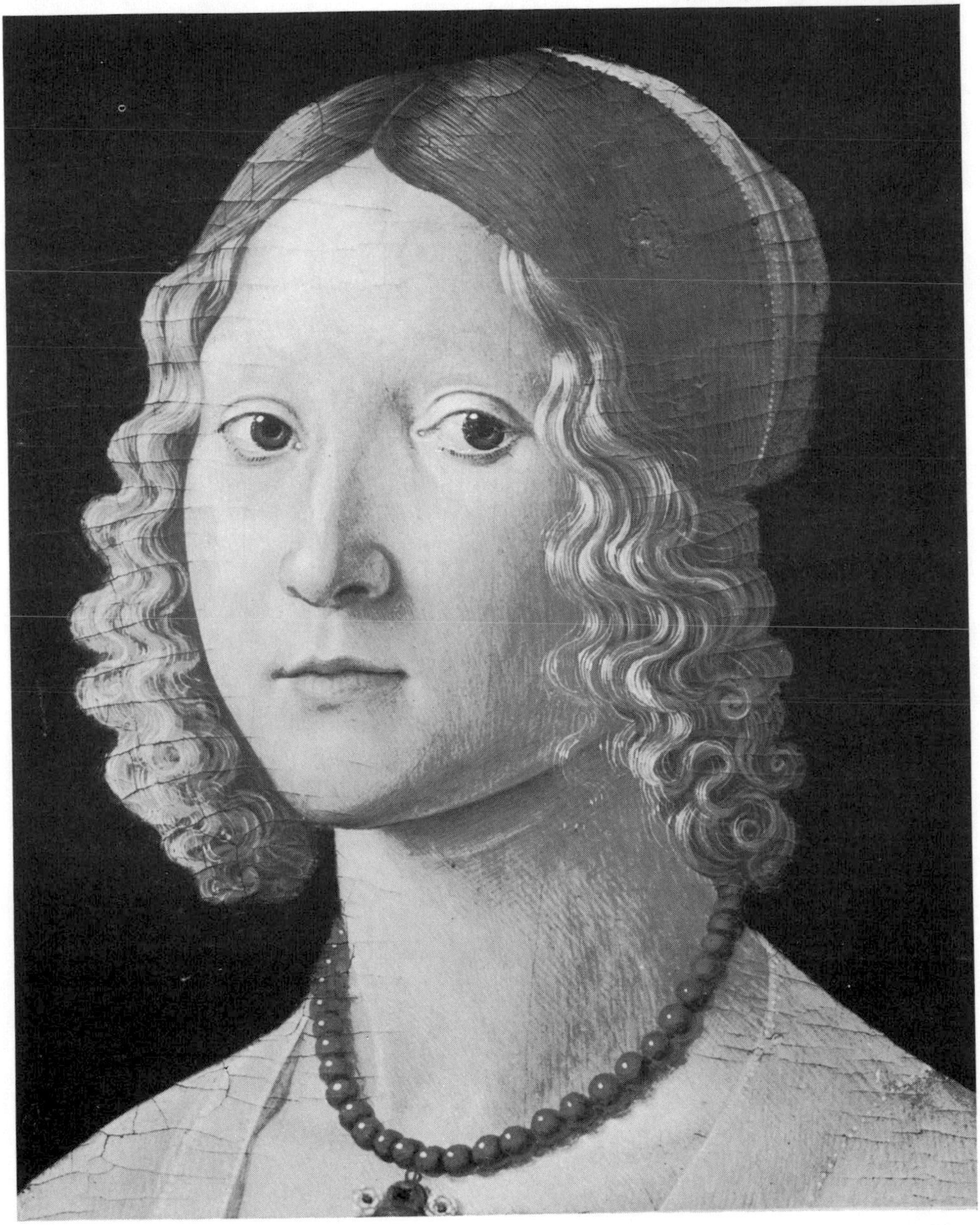

Fig. 13. Carlo Crivelli (active by 1457, died c. 1495). "Annunciation."

Fig. 13A. Detail from Crivelli's "Annunciation."

sarily to the extent of becoming careless, but he is likely to spend much less time in covering up the underpainting of the hands. We can see, therefore, that this thinner overpaint or semiglaze will yield more readily to the repeated cleaning given the painting throughout the centuries, especially the unscientific cleaning which was practiced in earlier days.

Antonello da Messina (1430?-1479). Sicilian. "Portrait of a Young Man," Figure 16

In contrast to Ghirlandaio's portrait in figure 12, the Flemish technique is very much in evidence here, though the artist is also Italian. The dark background is raised above the level of the face simply because white paint was not used with impasto for painting flesh. Instead, the light color of the flesh largely depended on the whiteness of the gesso ground. Although the face does not suggest the existence of an underpainting, a very light modeling, probably in pink color, most likely preceded the final painting. Had the painter worked directly over a white surface, the face would have had to be done alla prima, which, although unlikely, is yet a possibility. Let us explore the latter theory a little further. A thin shading of enamel-like smoothness such as seen in this portrait simply cannot be done in stages when using natural coloring from the start. However, had the painter worked from a drawing (that is, not directly from the model), an assumption which appears quite plausible, in a day's labor the painting of the face could very well have been done alla prima on the white gesso ground.

The fine threads of the hair are not raised, nor do they have the typically hard look of the tempera-in-oil paint.

Filippino Lippi (c.1457-1504). Florentine. "Madonna Adoring the Child, with an Angel" (Detail), Figure 17

An archaic workshop tradition guided Filippino in painting this Adoration scene. A pure tempera grisaille is evident in the body of the child. Whether this faintly hatched monotone was merely preparatory to glazing in full colors cannot be said, but it seems probable; it is also conceivable that the overpaint, or oil glazes, have been removed by cleaning at one time, and that what we see today is merely an underpainting.

The handling of the greens shows extraordinary beauty in color and texture. The entire carpet of leaves and flowers is painted in a high, plastic relief of enamel-like quality showing the highest perfection in craftsmanship. Modeled in several shades of dark green, such ornamentation can be produced only when painted wet-in-wet, that is, when one color is painted into another before the first one dries.

The effect which is not infrequently apparent in paintings of similar technique, is clearly registered in this detail. Going ever so slightly beyond the edge of the high impasto, a tone which softens the contour appears. This is caused, it would seem, by the vehicle which, while separating itself from the body of the paint, blurs the outline.

Joos van Cleve (?-1540). Flemish. "Crucifixion" (Detail), Figure 18

The quality of this painting is by no means inferior as regards the brush stroke, contour, and texture, but the state of preservation is poor due to the partial disintegration of the gesso priming which covers the wood panel. The minutiae in the panel are seen with a keen eye and executed with great deftness.

Again I am inclined to believe here that the details were executed with an aqueous tempera medium painted into wet oil. To realize the scale of the work, consider that the bridge at the top of the illustration is only an inch long in the original painting. Although the execution of such miniature renderings may limit the broadness of the painter's scope, if we think for instance of the more facile technique of Rubens, this should certainly not prevent us from delighting in the intrinsic beauty of such intimate passages.

Lucas Cranach (1472-1553). German. "Judgment of Paris," Figure 19

Although Cranach was a contemporary of Titian, one could hardly think of a greater contrast. In technique, the German painter appears to be a century behind the times. His, like others discussed in this chapter, is truly an archaic style. With a technique that adheres closely to handed-down workshop methods, we find once more in his work the combination of the tempera and oil medium, or so it would seem. If we compare the effects produced by the experiments in the tempera-in-oil technique (figure 2) they impress us as identical with the character of paint in the headdress and the jewelry shown in figure 19.

In the flesh parts, a network of deep cracks is visible as a result of the very thin painting on top of the gesso priming. These cracks end where the thick oil paint (used in the greens of the background) starts. Whether the cracks continue under the heavy background layer of paint is difficult to determine, but examination of the paint-

35

ing shows that the thick film, rich in oil, has retained its elasticity and cohesion through all these centuries.

The treatment of the foliage in the work of Cranach (as well as that of Altdorfer and some other painters of the same school) is most interesting and instructive. This effect is obtained by using oil paint of very heavy consistency and of a color representing the darkest accents. This is laid in with impasto. Into this viscous (wet but rather immobile) layer of paint, the design of the foliage—the twigs and branches—is painted in light colors with a stringy or long paint, using a pointed sable brush. By a "long" paint we mean a paint of high viscosity which is rather liquid, hence does not retain brush marks.

Perugino (1446-1523). Italian. "The Crucifixion, with the Virgin, Saint John, Jerome, and Mary Magdalene" (Detail), Figure 20

As a composition, this panel (or, to be exact, three panels, since the detail in figure 20 represents only a portion of the left wing of an altar triptych) witnesses to the painter's mastery. There is grandiloquence and imagination in the organization of the composition in its entirety which bespeaks great authority. However, in this particular example Perugino's method of painting though entirely in the medium of oil differs only slightly from the approach of the tempera painter who labored under much harder technical difficulties. As yet the greater freedom of expression exemplified by Titian, Tintoretto, and Raphael, to name three great examples, was yet to come. Although the treatment in this Crucifixion panel allows for neither the play of glazes nor the use of telling impasti, it is to be noted that Perugino discovered the much broader use of the oil medium when he painted the triptych "Virgin, Child, and Saints," which is in the National Gallery, London. Whereas the underpainting in the "Crucifixion" is scant and plays little part in the final effect, which is relatively flat, greater modeling is to be found in some other works which reflect the great advancement of technique after the turn of the fifteenth century.

Giovanni Bellini (1430?-1516). Venetian. "Saint Jerome Reading" (Detail), Figure 21

In an example such as this, the medium of paint can be said already to have become a symphonic language. Of course, poetic imagination has as much to do with the creation of a masterpiece as anything else, but the means or technique to enable it to be presented is equally necessary. In Bellini's "Saint Jerome," it is the nature of the resilient paint body that lends animation to the twigs, the leaves, and the grasses; the glazes form the stratification of rocks and make the colors appear now soft and mellow, now harsh and sinewy.

I have stood hours on end before Bellini's landscapes, trying to elicit the secret that breathes life into those stalks of flowers or weeds —and the nearest conclusion I could arrive at is that boiled oil and stringy paint are the substance of this aliveness. And I have my doubts whether Bellini himself, or anyone else for that matter, could do as well with the aluminum stearate color paste which comes nowadays from the tube.

Observe the archaism of his pictorial conception—the far-off castle across the water and the rabbits and leaves right in front of us, for example, are all kept in the same clear focus. Notwithstanding this precision of forms, the appearance of contours is not hard. I do not believe this mellowed effect is achieved entirely through the handling of the brush, but rather that the secret lies in the nature of the paints which, because of their higher fusibility, never create antagonistic borders. There is always a sensation of mutual permeability between the adjoining color areas.

Fig. 14. Michelangelo (1475–1564). "Madonna, Child, Saint John, and Angels."

Fig. 15. Lorenzo de Credi (1459–1537). "Portrait of a Lady."

39

Fig. 16. Antonello da Messina (1430–1479). "Portrait of a Young Man."

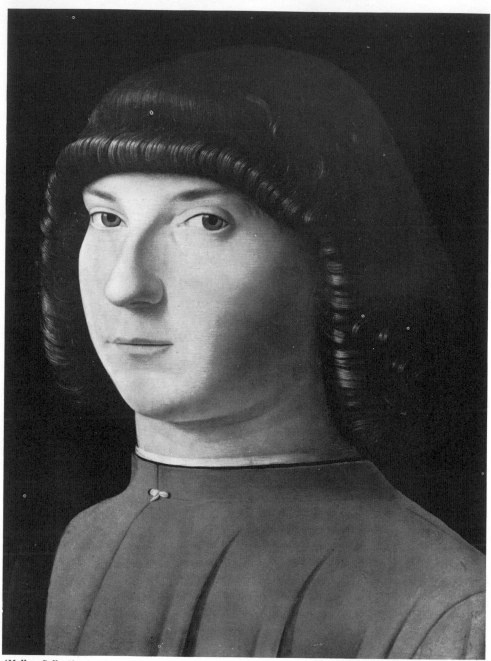

Fig. 17. Filippino Lippi (1457–1504). "Madonna Adoring the Child, with an Angel" (detail).

41

Fig. 19. Lucas Cranach (1472–1553). "Judgment of Paris" (detail).

Opposite page: Fig. 18. Joos van Cleve (d. 1540). "Crucifixion."

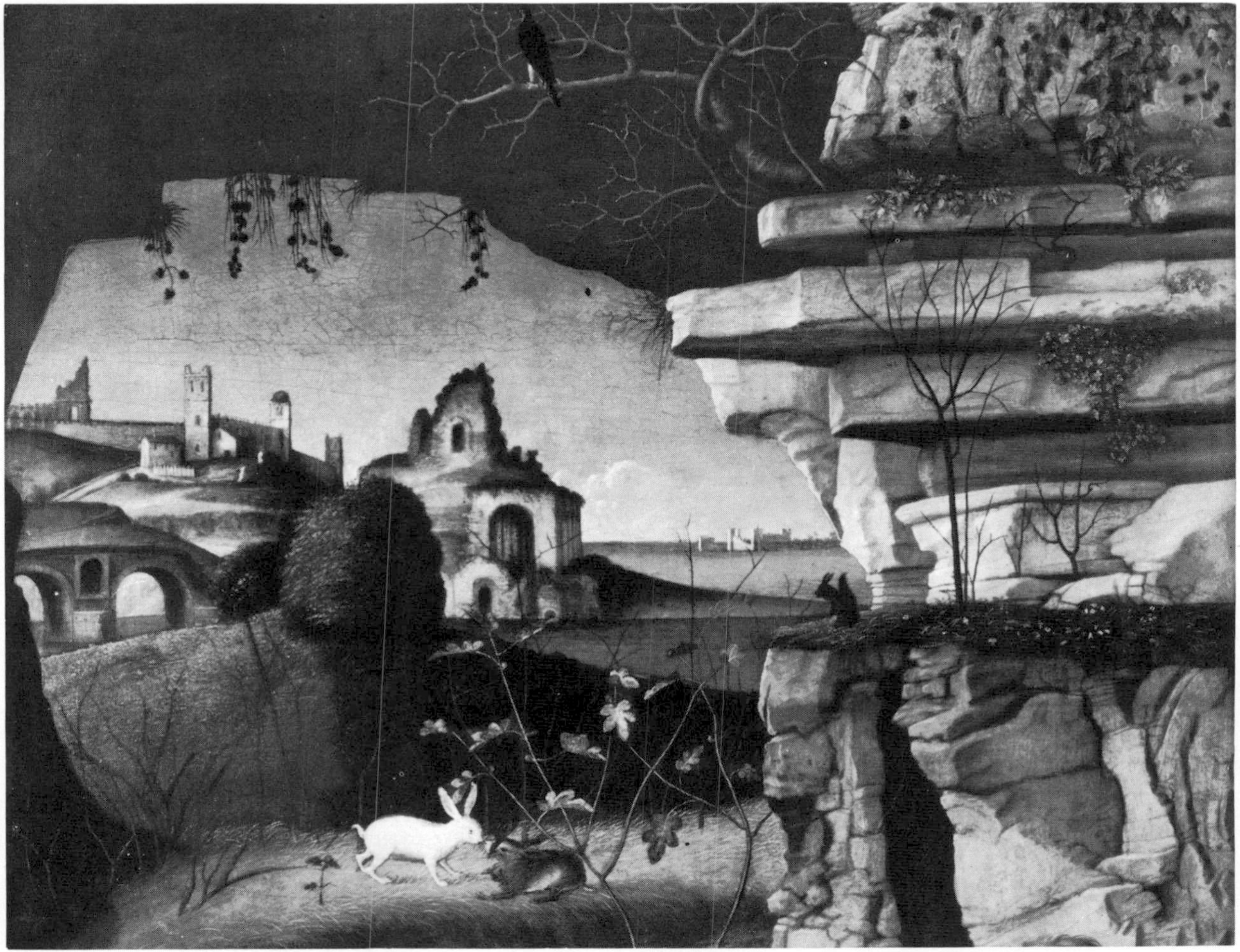

Fig. 21. Giovanni Bellini (c. 1430-1516). "Saint Jerome Reading" (detail).

5

RAPHAEL, TINTORETTO, RUBENS
A STUDY IN CONTRASTS

WITH THE PRIMITIVE conception of painting on the wane the Renaissance produced an astonishing quantity of great painters who, using the oil medium in preference to tempera, helped raise the standard of easel painting to its greatest heights. One can enumerate painters all the way from those who were first awakened to the possibilities of this versatile medium, such as Antonello da Messina (1430?-1479), who is said on the one hand to have borrowed from the discoveries of the Flemish originator van Eyck, and on the other to have discovered an oil medium of his own in Italy, up to those who developed it fully and without compromise, such as Titian (1477-1576), Raphael (1483-1520), Tintoretto (1518-1594), and later painters.

At this point we cannot be concerned with how each individual painter who used the oil medium developed his technique, for to take all the great masters of this period one by one would require several volumes; and not only would many of our conjectures be highly speculative, but there would be a great deal of repetitious material.

It may therefore not seem too arbitrary to take three of the greatest oil painters, two Italians and one Flemish, and study them together in this chapter. It might be noted that the dates of Raphael

46

(1483-1520), Tintoretto (1518-1594), and Rubens (1577-1640) show three different generations; each also represents a different school of painting. All these men worked with the oil medium and each, in his own way, has almost equal claim on posterity. While others in the galleries of the great follow later in the book, our chief reason for dealing with these three now is because their oil techniques make a very satisfactory study in contrasts.

The works of Raphael, who received his training in Perugia and Florence, are particularly distinguishable from those of Tintoretto, a Venetian follower of Titian in the manner of underpainting or, to be accurate, in the attention given the establishment of a *special* underpainting.

A superficial examination of these two painters and others who fall into the general category of one or the other will disclose conspicuous differences. The paint surface of Raphael's paintings is, quite often, in a poor condition (if we disregard the repaints of various restorers) and marked to a lesser or stronger degree by a variety of cracks. This is interesting because the paintings of Raphael's master, Perugino, are, on the whole, remarkably free from all signs of deterioration.

Now we know that already twenty years after Raphael's death, some of his works, then in France, required restoration. No lesser man than the painter Primaticcio was entrusted with this task.

Disregarding the probability that the damage suffered by the paintings (specifically by the glazes, according to a contemporary report) occurred on the occasion of a cleaning, we must conclude that the actual appearance of the paint surfaces of so many of his works points to a deeper seated cause. It would seem that perhaps not enough time was allowed for drying of the various underpaintings, and this may be the true reason for the condition. Moreover, there is no evidence that Raphael ever used a resin in his medium, which, in my opinion, would have facilitated the incorporation of the successive paint layers. Of course, there is the possibility of an excessive paint shrinkage that may have also played a role in causing certain characteristic cracks such as we see on many of the master's paintings.

Now, the Tintorettos (and Titians) are also in a poor condition, but for a different reason from the works of Raphael. In point of fact Tintoretto worked chiefly on a toned ground, he did not underpaint in the usual sense. It is quite probable that the deteriorations of the Venetian canvases are due partly to the humid and salty atmosphere of the geographic location. Also, the use of walnut oil—a favorite medium of the north Italian painters—should be considered in connection with the poor preservation, for the nut oil, as we know, does not form as tough a linoxyn as linseed oil or the still far

Fig. 22. Raphael (1483–1520). "The Small Cowper Madonna" (detail).

Fig. 23. *Tintoretto (1518–1594). "A Venetian Senator" (detail).*

Fig. 24. Tintoretto. "Doge Alvise" (detail).

Opposite page: Fig. 25. Tintoretto. "Christ at the Sea of Galilee."

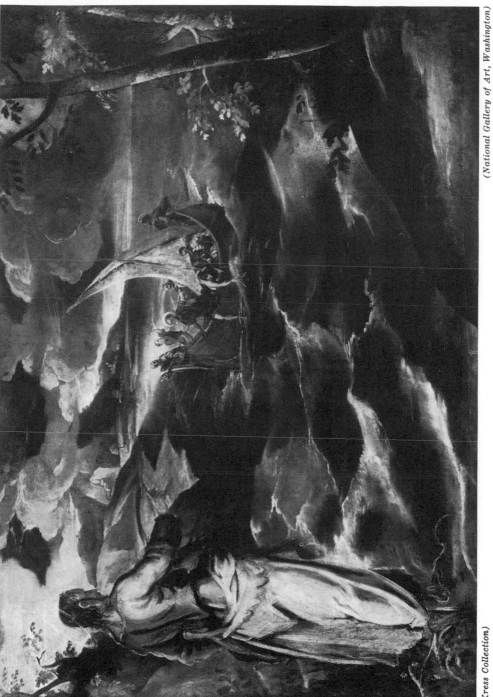

Fig. 26. Peter Paul Rubens (1577–1640). "Triumphal Entry of Henri IV" (detail).

Opposite page: Fig. 27. Rubens. "Ariadne on Naxos" (detail).

(Boyman's
Museum
Rotterdam)

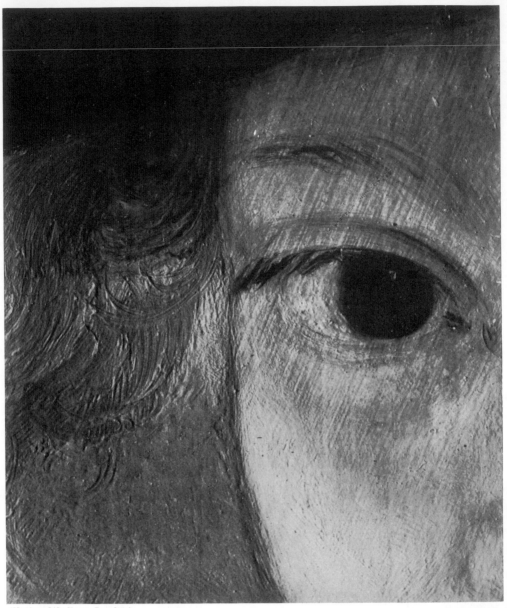

Fig. 28. Rubens. "The Straw Hat" (detail).

Fig. 29. Rubens. "Chateau de Steen."

Fig. 29A. Detail from the same picture.

more weather-resistant stand oil, the favorite of the painters in the Lowlands.

From what has been said, it may seem that the many underpaintings of Raphael, as contrasted with the practical lack of underpaintings that we see in the work of Tintoretto, is a partial cause of the ills attributed to Raphael's work. This, assuredly, is not the case. On the contrary, heavy underpaintings, when properly executed, may become the backbone of a painting and thus safeguard its permanence. Whereas one thin layer of paint may simply wear out in the course of centuries, a "skin" many times thicker may have a better chance of surviving by having greater resistance to all kinds of vicissitudes, such as continued "light" cleaning or an occasional varnish removal and the customary thorough cleaning by means of strong solvents.

As to the importance of a sound underpainting, let us digress a moment and see what Dürer said on the subject in a letter dated 1509: "Of ordinary pictures I will paint a pile which no one will believe it possible for one man to do it in such a short time." Now I am well acquainted with Dürer's published letters and, being a painter myself, I recognize the "sales talk" this master was wont to dispense when writing to his patrons and prospective clients. So when he asserts that a painting ordered from him is not "ordinary," it might seem that this, too, is perhaps a mere sales talk. However, there are really two kinds of Dürers: works done alla prima, like the one of King Christian of Denmark, for example, which, as we read in the master's *Travel Diary on the Trip to the Netherlands,* was done while changing stage coaches, as it were, in a matter of hours; and then, again, those—to use his own words— ". . . painted with good ultramarine, under, and over, and over that again, some five or six times . . ." He refers here of course to many layers of underpainting, which he assures his patron will last for "five hundred years."

Rubens' technique—so Flemish in character, hence so different from that of the Italian masters—falls into two distinct categories, which we may call formal and informal. The formal pictures, especially those in monumental scale, really represent the teamwork of his assistants and carry only his characteristic retouchings. The small panels on the other hand fully reveal the intimate touch of the master's hand. When we speak of teamwork, it must be pointed out that the design was always the master's own, but was merely "blown up" by the helpers.

The distinction between the large and the small panels lies also in the fact that, whereas the former were underpainted, the latter always carried an imprimatura. The underpainting was chiefly a "factory" work and it was carried out to a point where, with the least amount of effort, the master could put onto them his characteristic signature. These differences of technique between the larger and the small works are not arbitrary. The intimate, breezy work of the small canvases would look decidedly empty and anemic if enlarged to mural proportions.

Let us now examine works by these three masters in turn.

Raphael. "The Small Cowper Madonna," Figure 22 (Detail)

It is not merely a legend that Raphael's art towered above that of his contemporaries, nor—as some of the contemporaries had it—was his industry, more than his genius, the mainstay of his art. Now it would be easy for us to invoke his sense of ordered design, his infallible taste, and great charm (a word now under strictest esthetic embargo) in order to uphold our verdict of his superiority, but we shall confine ourselves to the mechanics of the brush alone, which in Raphael is art of the highest order. Here every component of the painting is well considered and taken care of in the underpainting.

To realize the care that was given to the building up of the "Cowper Madonna," observe, for example, the small segment of cloth under the Child's right arm and framing the Madonna's shoulder. Because it was meant to receive a different treatment from the flesh it is on a much higher level. This might seem like a trivial observation but it is indicative of the methodical procedure that went into the making of such paintings.

With painstaking exactness, Raphael (or, we should rather say, his assistants) prepared an underpainting according to a well-thought-out plan. The parts to be glazed (or, at any rate, to be finished in thin paint) were plastically raised above the level of the flesh which, according to tradition, was to derive its luminosity from the underlying gesso, and was hence modeled thinly in a warm monotone. The area of the sky, for example, is so thickly underpainted that the marks of the halos have been indented in the stratum of paint.

A precision in the ultimate finish necessitates a relative smoothness of the underpainting. For the artist to have achieved the Raphaelesque "super-finish," the edges in the underpainting must already have shown soft transitions so as to facilitate the blending in the overpaint. These contours of the finished painting also indicate, for the most part, the existence of a rather thin final layer of paint, for impasti do not lend themselves to a meticulous blending of edges. Aside from these observable considerations, we know that much of the glazing on his paintings, damaged in the process of cleaning, had to be restored as early as the middle of the sixteenth century.

Tintoretto. "A Venetian Senator" (Detail), Figure 23. "Doge Alvise" (Detail), Figure 24. "Christ at the Sea of Galilee," Figure 25

The surface of "A Venetian Senator" is in a relatively fair present condition but, having been relined and renovated, it is a difficult one to read. The white paint had a good degree of viscosity and that fact can still be seen in the painting of the fur at the edge of the red coat (figure 23). From this part of the painting we learn also that the underpainting must have been of a grayish color, at least in this area.

The deft strokes of the brush as seen on the sleeve of the coat are part of a freely handled grisaille, on top of which madder lake, strengthened in the shadows with black, was applied. To make these bold strokes (which indicate the pattern of the folds) stand out, the painter simply wiped off the madder paint with a rag. This was quite easy, for these strokes are the only ones standing out in impasto. When the color is wiped off, some of it always remains embedded in the crevices and interstices of the paint conformation and thus it aids in "pulling together" all the glazed areas.

On this detail we can also realize how ancient are the means of the painter's language, how early they were understood and used to the best advantage. The little lagoon in the background and the sailboats are all treated in open color. The color of the sea represents the middle tone. To define the objects in lights, the painter simply high-lighted them with white; then he brushed some darker, rather neutral color lightly on top of the middle tone to accentuate the plastic form.

In the "Doge Alvise," Tintoretto showed a different technique by simplifying his method to the most elementary and essential utterances. Drawing with the brush—in this instance it appears to have been a bristle brush—is the gist of the technique shown in figure 24, and it is responsible for the impression of vigor and great spontaneity. Objects are treated, regardless of their importance, as if they were no more than marginal accessories. It is from such examples that much of modern art derives its license and inspiration. Because a great deal of the painting remains as a mere sketch, the imagination of the observer is kept alive, trying to discover what has been left unsaid.

The open-color technique calls for the simplest form of underpainting, preferably a toned ground, showing, perhaps, some variations here and there. Upon such a foundation the painter treated the objects in a draftsmanlike fashion and pushed the possibilities of this technique to its ultimate limits. Thus the color belonging to the palace in the background goes right through the hand of the figure held in midair. The color of the lute is identical with that of the figure holding it. This allowed the painter to indicate with the barest of lines the shape of the instrument. A similar approach is evident in all the other expositions of the painting.

The large canvas "Christ at the Sea of Galilee" (figure 25) also shows a short-hand technique. The entire canvas is covered with a brownish imprimatura, and there is no underpainting save in the robe of the Christ which, because it is painted in madder lake, carries a grisaille extremely loose in treatment.

Although there is very little open color in this painting, the aid of light and dark outlines is made ample use of to strengthen the design and lend to it a feeling of animation.

I have on several occasions emphasized the importance of using proper tools in the realization of a pictorial expression. Paintings such as the example we have just examined could not suffer a soft hair brush of any kind, even for linear definition. The nature of the support, mostly coarse in texture and not well covered by either priming or underpainting, as well as his particular coloristic treatment, called for a relatively stiff bristle brush to the exclusion of all other instruments.

Rubens. "Triumphal Entry of Henry IV" (Detail), Figure 26. "Ariadne on Naxos," Figure 27. "The Straw Hat" (Detail), Figure 28. "Chateau de Steen," Figures 29 and 29A

As was Rubens' custom, the small gessoed panel was first covered with a yellowish, streaky imprimatura over which the painting was carried out alla prima. Or, perhaps, instead of "painting" we should refer rather to colored delineations. However, a procedure such as this cannot be classified as "colored painting" in the sense of the early Flemish masters, for here drawing and coloring are done in one operation.

In works such as the "Triumphal Entry" Rubens employed the simplest form of glazing technique which, however, does not utilize a multicolored underpainting to influence the color of the glazes. In keeping with the sketchy character of the work, the imprimatura remains uncovered in many spots throughout the panel, thus joining the fragmentary statements to a homogeneous fabric.

These small Rubens panels are very numerous. I examined a large number of them at the Boymans Museum in Rotterdam, (including the one of which a detail is shown in figure 27), at the Wallace Collection, and a number in other museums both here and abroad. I cannot agree with those who say that these sketchy works were underpainted. The semitransparent surface, in most of them at least, reveal to me a one-phase operation, and it is in the nature of spontaneous rendition that it be done without a preliminary underpainting.

Even the portrait reproduced in the much enlarged detail photo (figure 28) does not seem to have a layer of paint under the final painting; it has only the characteristic streaky, diagonally brushed-on imprimatura which permits the white gesso ground underneath to assert itself clearly. The imprimatura is revealed much more distinctly in the photo than in the original work. Also, it is to be noted that the area adjoining the face is not as pastose in the original as it appears in this illustration. This painting, too, was in my opinion largely a one-phase operation.

In contrast to these small panels and the portrait, the landscape, "Chateau de Steen," shown in detail in figures 29 and 29A, is a painting of considerable size. Here as well as in a similar work in the Wallace Collection, Rubens did not employ the gray, yellowish, or brownish undertone we are accustomed to see in his figure pieces but a rather dark burnt sienna imprimatura. Among the flowers reproduced in figure 29A, this warm tone remains uncovered in a few places, and keeps recurring elsewhere in the landscape. Presumably the entire panel was covered with the glowing imprimatura, in the absence of any systematic underpainting. Whatever undercoats of solid paint appear in this work, they should be considered unsatisfactory paint passages which required corrective paint layers.

6

PIETER BRUEGHEL, THE ELDER (1521?-1569)

In a later chapter I refer at length to Rembrandt's technique and point out the difference between the characteristic of his work and that of his contemporaries. An analogous case is, we may say, that of the Flemish painter Brueghel the Elder and the painters of his time. There is as much difference between a Brueghel and a van Cleve, for example, as there is between a Rembrandt and a Maes.

In the masters of the Flemish School, almost identical shop methods were employed throughout the century by Bosch, Patinir, Quentin Matsys, and van Cleve, for instance. While Brueghel followed the same principles, his craftsmanship has a definite character of its own. I am not considering here a "personal" manner of brush stroke but rather the physical character of paint application. There is an incredible delicacy of touch with a "genius" such as Brueghel in contrast to a certain heavy-handedness apparent in the talents of lesser men of his day. This delicacy of technique is not to be confused with the boldness of Brueghel's conception when painting his coarse rustic characters.

I have mentioned on several occasions my preference for heavy impasti, and I have suggested that glazes—abundant glazes, to be precise—may enfeeble the painter's language. Although this holds true in most instances, where the painter displays abilities in various degrees, it does not apply to men of genius. Out of the delicate glazes in Brueghel's paintings there arises an elemental energy that does not need to seek support in forceful impasti.

The "inner light" of such panels as the "Harvesters," a detail of which is seen in figure 30, arises from the cold white gesso (covered

61

Fig. 30. Pieter Brueghel (1520?–1569). "The Harvesters"
(detail). See full picture in color section.

Fig. 31. Pieter Brueghel. "Parable of the Sower" (detail).

in this instance with an ocherish imprimatura) upon which the painting is spread in a fashion that amounts to glazing or semiglazing at best. Only the "soupy" greens are always opaque and, when placed in the foreground, as in the foliage of trees, quite pastose.

In figure 30 the original size of the central figure measures about five inches. Here there is not a trace of individuality of brush stroke, and we seek in vain for a message relayed through a characteristic handwriting elsewhere. Except for a masterly spatial organization of the composition, very personal and ingenious in design, there is nowhere a display of pictorial fireworks to be found. How could it be otherwise? The panel, over six feet in length, was obviously painted with a small water-color brush!

In the "Parable of the Sower" (figure 31) the "light touch" referred to previously is especially evident. With the exception of the dense greens, all the colors show transparency in various degrees. Under the rock toward the front of this detail, for example, in the areas of the shadows, a transparent green appears, glazed over a pink underpainting. Also, the underpainting proper is not quite opaque, for the white color of the gesso is felt throughout the entire panel. Hence the pictorial utterances which create the characteristic Brueghelesque mood are interlocked in subtle, misty glazes. They enveil the valleys and precipitous ravines and cast an enigmatic spell over the scene.

The alacrity of touch which may be responsible for these effects should not be mistaken for skill; the "touch" is really a matter of spirit—of buoyancy and volatility of mood. Here it is the intellectual content which rules over the material elements.

7

REMBRANDT AND HALS

MUCH HAS BEEN WRITTEN on the subject of the physical quality of the paint in Rembrandt's surfaces. They are most characteristic and were not even approximated by his pupils.

The most accurate and acceptable theory is that Rembrandt's paint was compounded with stand oil, with or without the addition of hard resin. Indeed, stand oil originated in Holland long before Rembrandt's time and was the generally accepted material.

I do not agree with A. P. Laurie, who refers to Rembrandt's white as stiff and not flowing; nor can I go along with his assertion that Rembrandt had a secret which he did not reveal to his pupils, and the further suggestion that whiting may have been added to the white lead to produce the particular quality that we find in Rembrandt's impasti. Rembrandt's white is not stiff (that is, short); on the contrary, it is always long. White lead will be extra short if compounded with a minimum (9 to 10 per cent) of unpolymerized oil and it can be stiffened to a consistency of semihardened putty by using means less outlandish than whiting—a drop of a high acid varnish, for instance.

Effects that we so admire in Rembrandt's paintings are always executed in flowing, long color. This in itself is not unique, for such a characteristic is common in Dutch painting. The difference between Rembrandt's painting and that of his followers—Maes (see figure 44), Bol, Fabritius, and others—lies in the manner of application rather than in the type of paint used. It is Rembrandt's audacity in the build-up of his impasti, and not a secret of his paint formulation, that produces the miraculous web of his textures. A master of Rembrandt's creative impetuosity simply charged his canvases in a manner in which a less inspired and knowing hand would not dare, for it would have lost itself in a jungle of viscous paint layers, thus ending up in what could best be described as an "unholy mess."

Of course, when we speak of Rembrandt's characteristic technique, we think of his mature efforts when he discarded traditional methods and expressed himself with complete freedom.

In its broad aspects his manner of painting differed from that of the earlier painters inasmuch as it relied more on improvisation than on prearranged planning. Whereas the compositions of the latter tended to have been carefully laid out and then meticulously followed, it looks as though Rembrandt may even have surprised himself by the final effects he achieved. This does not imply that the early painters committed themselves irrevocably to an originally predetermined plan. Departures from such a plan, to a minor or larger extent, can be seen in the works of Titian, Rubens, Velasquez, and others. Also from recent X-ray photographs of paintings by Bronzino and Veronese we detect that the apparent unerring drafts manship was not so impeccable to begin with, for the photographs reveal marked deviations from the original designs.

However, on the whole we must say that in a technique which employs glazes and semiglazes—in other words, where the underpainting does not disappear under a heavy layer of paint—there is not much opportunity for improvisations, or at least for repeated pictorial restatements.

Our first and strongest impression of the technique of Rembrandt (1606-1669) is what might be called a boldness of handwriting. Up to now we have scrutinized many painting surfaces, but Rembrandt's are different. They are unique with crags, crevices, hillocks, and declivities, which, in total, produce the extraordinarily powerful and penetrating effects on canvas that distinguish his genius.

It is illuminating to contrast the forceful approach as seen in the head of Lucretia (figure 32) with the elegance of Gainsborough's head of Mrs. Elliott, reproduced later in the book (figure 62). In painting the "Lucretia," Rembrandt's brushes could be called, without too much exaggeration, brooms. Observe the strokes dividing the lips and the slash marking the nostrils. Surely Mrs. Elliott's refined nostrils would have been gravely offended by similar treatment. Gainsborough, with fastidious patrons of eighteenth-century England to please, chose a delicate sable brush terminating in a precise needle point with which he could caress the lady's features and just sweep over the parted lips as if with the touch of a butterfly's wings. Compare the feathery fluff of the glazed hair with the plastically raised impasto of Lucretia's headdress. Rembrandt chose to let the extreme impasto (made of a dense dark paint, "soupy" enough not to leave clear imprints of a brush) stand out on an equally dark background. His wish must have been to have the tangible substance of the hair materialize itself in space—the empty background.

In examining the head in figure 33 and the photo-micrograph (figure 33A) from the surface of the self-portrait, the characteristic of his impasto can more clearly be visualized. In a pictorial conception such as was Rembrandt's, the impasto and the linear treatment are incompatible.

It is to be noted that on a great many of Rembrandt's paintings the impasto texture has been more or less flattened out by improper treatment on the occasion of relining. These relinings were done, for the most part, in the nineteenth century when the technique of restoration was not perfected and the problems of conservation not well understood. On the "Lady with a Pink," for instance, in the Metropolitan Museum of Art, the impasti, with the exception of the painting in of the jewelry, are moderate. This may be due to a forceful pressing of the canvas at the time of the relining.

In the painting "The Toilet of Bathsheba" (figure 34), which was done when the master was forty years old, the figure must have been underpainted several times. The impasto was first laid in heavily with a stiffer brush; next, as we see from the somewhat pebbly surface, this thick impasto was well swept together with a soft-hair blender. The same treatment was accorded to the contours of the figure which meet the equally thickly painted background in a blend of softly flowing and interlaced brush strokes.

A similar impasto treatment appears on "The Circumcision" in the National Gallery of Art, Washington, where on the robe of the priest the brush deposited a maze of softly flowing textures, such as can be produced in a lead color only—white lead, naples yellow, and especially the lead-tin yellow. All the native characteristics of the latter seem to appear on this mellow, sumptuous surface.

The photomicrograph (figure 33A), depicting a portion of paint from Rembrandt's self-portrait, reveals a surface where little or no blending was attempted. The brush marks here crisscross in several heavy overpaints. The nature of the colors—as we find them in most of Rembrandt's characteristic works—is that of high fusability, which implies that their viscosity must have been considerable. Yet in spite of their limpidness, the brush strokes preserve their identity, regardless of the tendency to merge and to seek a level, as is the nature of long paint.

In Rembrandt's portraits, whether the treatment is smooth and mellow or as rough as in the self-portrait, there is never a reliance on draftsmanlike effects. Even the contours of the eyelids, the marks of the eyebrows, or details such as one would ordinarily dispose of

67

by outlining are treated in a painterly manner, and they all evidence a handwriting the like of which cannot be found in any conventional portraiture. It is not a bravura that speaks here but a complete understanding of the medium of oil paint. When I say that a painting by Rembrandt does not evidence bravura—or, I should rather say, facility—this is true in general but not in all instances. In the details from the "Polish Rider," (figures 35 and 35A) an extraordinary bravura produces all the effects alla prima. It appears that most of this large canvas is an alla prima work, executed on a dark, brownish-gray toned ground. (I shall remind the reader that "alla prima," in the sense in which I interpret it, implies that the painter aims from the start to achieve the final effects in *one operation*. A toned ground or an imprimatura does not change the definition.)

As for the "Polish Rider," the underpainting in many places serves as the painting proper, which can be, in fact, looked upon as a technique in open color. The drawing that goes into such a treatment is, as it mostly appears in Rembrandt, painterly and not graphic— none of the lines remind one of drawing. Note the leg of the horse (the one in shade), the contouring of the other leg, and the slashes in black color defining the structure of the ground. In these parts the shadows were not painted, as were the lights, for much of the shadow area is part of the underpainting.

The same effect can be seen in the rider's hand holding the reins (figure 35A). The spontaneity of the execution shows up in the "drag" of the brush which, traveling in one single stroke over the rough ground, marks the reins. The utter economy of means is the beholder's delight, and the treatment of the raiment, the horse's head, and the right leg are such as one never finds in meticulously finished painting. In such works the master's most characteristic handwriting is apparent with but a few fleeting brush strokes on the monotone of the underpainting.

The "Woman Bathing' is also an alla prima painting. The detail reproduced in figure 36 shows the master's temperament more clearly, perhaps, than does any other of the details. We find ourselves carried away by the tremendous gusto of the brushwork, luxuriating, as it were, in the viscous paint. The brownish middle tone was purposely left uncovered on the wrist of the woman and on the edge of the shirt (and in other places not seen in the detail), thus permitting a clear reading of the painting's progress. It is a curious fact that this middle tone, visible as a half shadow on the wrist, was at one time overpainted in more recent times to "correct" a supposed deficiency. The overpaint came off on the occasion of a recent cleaning, whereupon strong remonstrances were heard from various quarters that the painting had been "ruined" by overcleaning. Only com-

68

plete ignorance of Rembrandt's technique could have sponsored such a statement, for the overpainting was quite obviously not done by his hand.

"The Concord of the States" (figure 37), which is obviously a commissioned work done most likely as a sketch for an engraving, can be considered a drawing done with paint. Here the color of the ground remains uncovered in the two horses in the foreground, in the lower foreground on the right side, and in many other areas in the background. This dark brown ground was given a faint modeling in identical but somewhat darker umber color made up of a thick paint (prepared with stand oil) in which all the other delineaments were carried out. The rest of the picture received light scumbles or was high-lighted with a pastose, strongly polymerized white color, thus leaving the painting in the condition of a typical monotone. An identical treatment can be seen in the two Rembrandts in the National Gallery in London, the "Deposition" and *Christ before Pilate.*"

The next three details from "Lucretia" (figures 38, 39, and 40) I consider to be a complete lesson in the use of the medium of oil paint. They demonstrate a boldness and ingenuity on the part of the artist such as none of the experimentalists since his day has ever equaled. We can see how the final painting was arrived at after tortuous processes of painting, overpainting, changes, and reversals of the initial plan. The texture of the underpainting and the overpaint appear to be at cross purposes. But the means belie the end result, for the apparent indecision and search culminate in a perfect resolution. Any seeming change of intentions obviously cannot be looked upon as anything but an intrinsic part of the master's technique.

It might be pertinent to quote a recent statement made by a well-known philosopher who, in his late eighties, came to the not too startling conclusion that all is not as simple as he had once believed. Now one need not necessarily reach four score and ten to arrive at a point where things do not appear simple at all, and every utterance, no matter how true, needs to be contradicted to emerge eventually as the truth. Such a synthesis is implicit in the fabric of some of Rembrandt's mature work.

To return to the details in figures 39 and 40, they are, I believe, the first such photographs to give a complete and clear exposition of the use of a palette knife in conjunction with brush strokes. On the sleeve of the arm in figure 39 we see a dense web, a quarrel, as it were, between the brush and the knife, each of the instruments seeking dominance and attempting to forge a statement. Here glazes superimposed with the keen blade of the knife riding roughshod

69

Fig. 32. Rembrandt (1606–1669). "Lucretia."

Fig. 32A. Rembrandt. "Lucretia" (detail).

Fig. 33. Rembrandt. "Portrait of Himself" (detail).

72

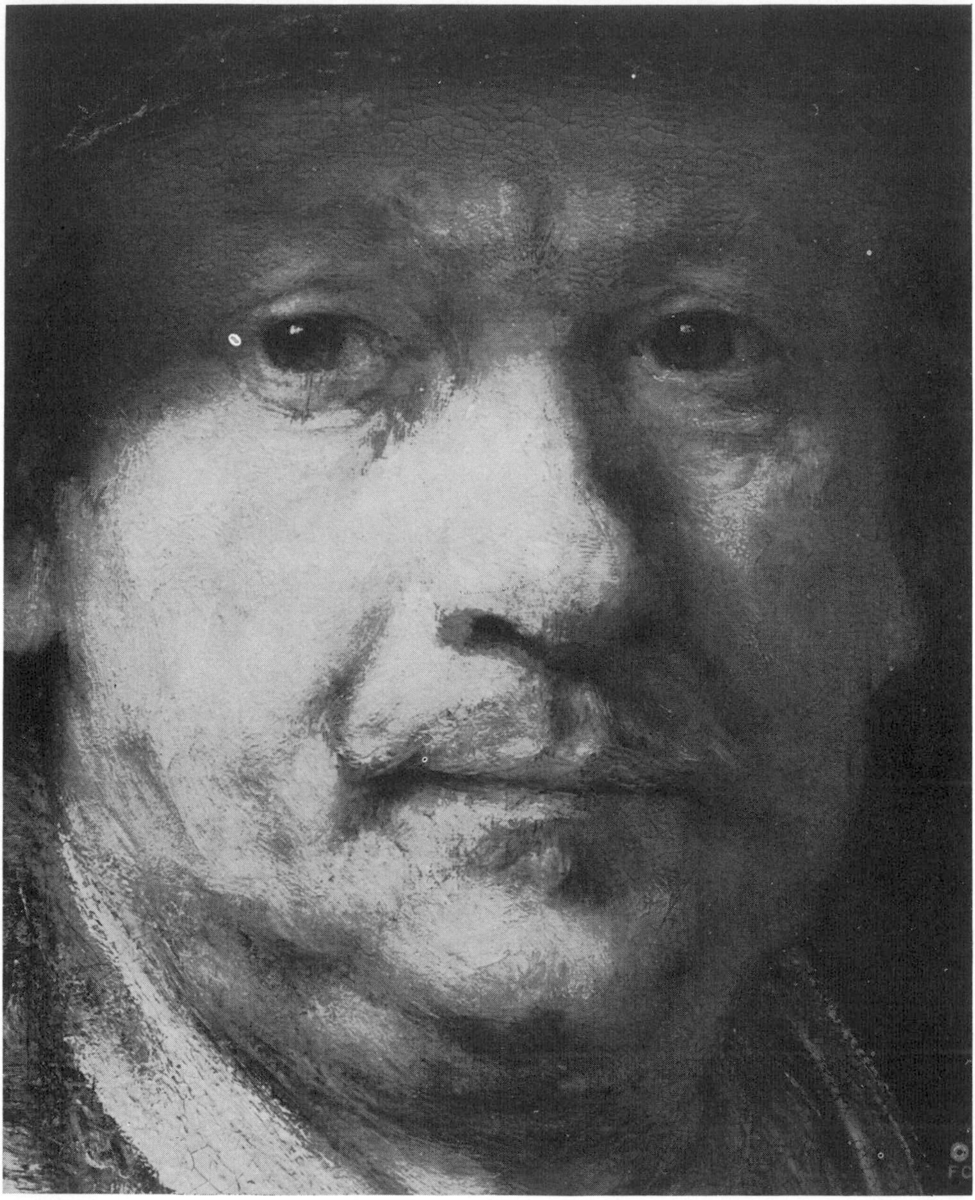

Fig. 33A. Rembrandt. "Portrait of Himself" (detail of nose). See also Fig. 33 on opposite page.

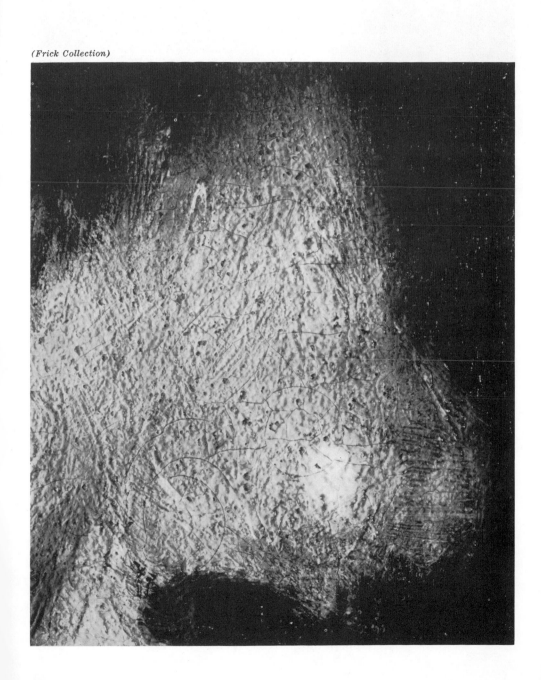

Fig. 34. Rembrandt. "The Toilet of Bathsheba" (detail).

Opposite page: Rembrandt. "The Polish Rider" (detail).

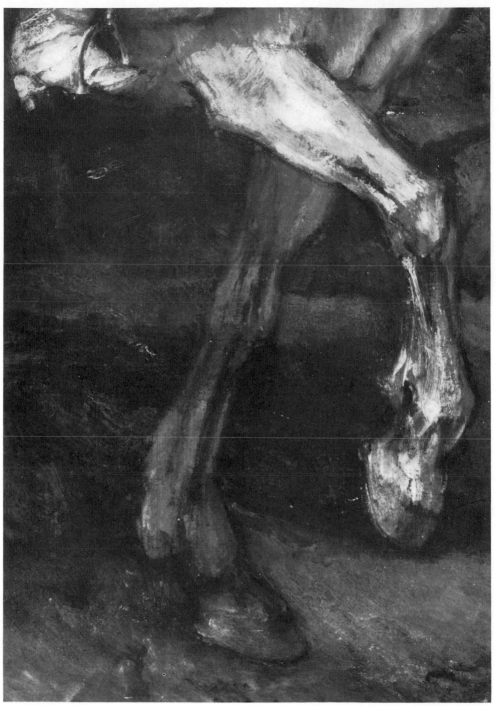

Fig. 35.

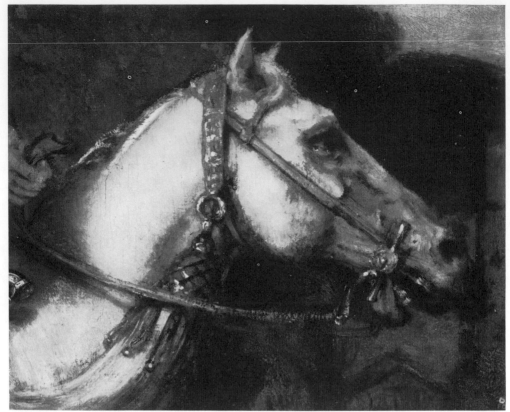

Fig. 35A. Rembrandt. "The Polish Rider" (detail).

Fig. 36. Rembrandt. "Woman Bathing" (detail).

(National Gallery, London)

(Boymans Museum, Rotterdam)

Fig. 37. Rembrandt. "The Concord of the States" (detail).

Fig. 38. Rembrandt. "Lucretia." Detail from the same painting shown on page 70.

Fig. 39.

Fig. 40.

*Figs. 39 and 40. Rembrandt. "Lucretia." Two more details
from the painting shown on page 70. Fig. 41. Detail of shirt
from the same painting.*

Fig. 42. Rembrandt. "The Sibyl" (detail).

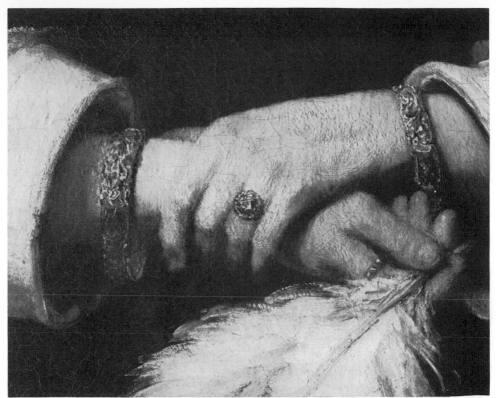

p. 83
Top: Rembrandt.
"Portrait of a Lady
with an Ostrich-
Feather Fan" (detail).
Bottom: Nicolaes
Maes(1632–1693)."An
Old Woman Dozing
over a Book" (detail).

Fig. 45. Frans Hals (1580?–1666). "Balthasar Coymans" (detail).

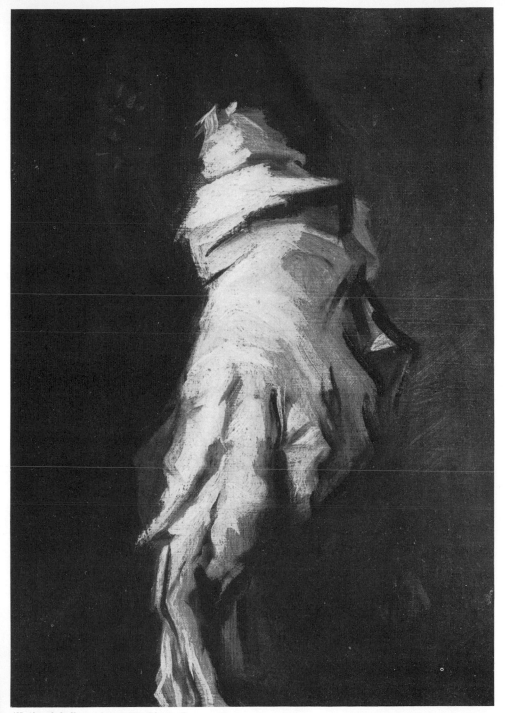

Fig. 46. Frans Hals. "Portrait of a Man" (detail).

over the maze of the impasto create an atmosphere of mystery. With apparent unconcern the painter starts off with a fully loaded brush and lets the impasto dry. Over this impasto a palette knife moves swiftly, later on to be modified with the brush again.

In figures 39 and 40, it appears, the knife carried glazes—an utterly unorthodox procedure and one not encountered in any other master painter's technique. (Goya's palette knife work was never used for glazing.) If today such a technique does not impress us as novel, it should be remembered that textural improvisations such as we encounter in Rembrandt's work were creative inventions of the master and wholly his own. The boldness of later-day painters in this respect relies on precedent. Thus, as always, a one-time audacity becomes, in the end, another pragmatic convention.

In figure 41, representing a section of the shirt, the character of the texture is puzzling, for the natural fall of the material is not defined by vertical strokes alone, as one would expect; but a network of small diagonal and horizontal brush strokes interferes. That it is just this puzzling network which alleviates the stark, plain square of the shirt, adorned merely with the chain strung obliquely across it, is evident.

The next detail, from the "Sybil," figure 42, represents a light impasto applied on top of a dark ground with knife and brush work alternating rapidly.

An extraordinary relief, built up undoubtedly from successive impasti, is seen on the bracelet from the "Lady with Fan," figure 43. To create such a plastic effect in one operation would be quite difficult—but not impossible. However, it would take many months for the heavy paint application to dry throughout, in contrast to only a few weeks when a few thin strata are superimposed. Once the heavy underpainting is dry, the design of the ornaments can be easily produced by means of the stringy, or long, paint.

One of Rembrandt's best-known pupils was Nicolaes Maes. The painting "Old Woman," a detail of which is shown in figure 44, belongs, no doubt, with his best performances. Nevertheless, it would be futile to compare the fabric of this painting to that of Rembrandt's, for Maes's inertia in matters of paint texture is much too apparent. However, let us parallel the hands as seen in the two details illustrated in figures 43 and 44. I have mentioned the painting of the hands purposely, for Rembrandt on the whole does not show particular distinction in painting of hands—but even in this instance the contrast is quite marked. At once we understand that an inert technique cannot very well produce an expression of intensity or even a semblance of life.

Holland of course produced a host of excellent painters, yet as subjects of my analyses I have chosen to dwell on the two most interesting ones from a painter's point of view—Rembrandt and Frans Hals (1580?-1666). They were contemporaries in an age when deviation in style was rather narrow, yet the disparity of their technical approach is very great.

In contrast to Rembrandt's laborious method which we have analyzed at some length, Frans Hals appeared to be a "dead shot" with his brush—an artist who hardly needed to take time even to aim. Yet he achieved the most difficult feats with a bravura probably never equaled since.

With a restricted palette, limited to less than ten colors, the eloquence of Hals's pictorial language relies, in the main, on articulation of the brush strokes alone. That such a spontaneity of execution calls for acute observation and instantaneous grasp of surface effects goes without saying. In other words, the chief force in the artist is the desire to circumscribe an immediately comprehended fact. Such a faculty of the highest order was alive in Hals. Take, for example, his painting of hands. No one before or after him understood how to present with greater speed and persuasiveness the inherent vitality of hands in all their interminable expressions. As I have stated before in my writings, imagination is the least and observation the most important faculty when it comes to painting of hands.

In a technique such as employed by Hals, no need for an elaborate underpainting exists. All effects emanate from the top stratum, for there is nothing to uphold them save a flimsy imprimatura, or a moderately thin toned ground.

In Hal's painting "Balthasar Coymans," as in most of his canvases employing a sketchy technique, we find a cool, brownish imprimatura-covered priming. (It is possible that the same kind of priming exists under the more elaborate works, but because of the entirely opaque top surface no definite conclusions can be made.) Even the term "imprimatura" appears, perhaps, not quite correct, for it could as well be an extra-thin toned ground. It is really the degree of transparency or opacity that determines the classification. In Frans Hals's paintings the degree of transparency is such that it might fit into both these classifications, for the underlying paint film is exceedingly thin and only semitransparent. Such paint can be produced by means of a diluent, or paint of normal consistency can be scraped so thinly with a palette knife as to resemble imprimatura. Aside from these considerations, the practicing painter will remember that imprimatura is produced without the admixture of white, whereas a toned ground will, in most cases, contain white lead paint.

Now let us follow, step by step, the painting of the detail shown

87

in figure 45. On the brownish imprimatura (as we shall call it hence-forth, because of its thinness), corresponding in value to the middle tone (that is, a tone which mediates, as it were, between the lights and the shadows), a gray scumble was spread onto the area of the shirt sleeve. This gray more or less approximates the value of the shadow. Then the shadows were strengthened here and there with a darker gray. Next, into the (wet) gray color the lights were painted with bold strokes of a round sable brush, and finally the few darkest accents were delineated in black color, all, of course, while painting wet-in-wet.

An identical procedure was employed in the painting of the hand: First, middle tone; next, deeper shadows; then, lights; and, finally, the darkest definitions.

The brocade of the coat sleeve is marked in extra-long lead-tin yellow painted into the wet gray color with impasto, and strength-ened in places with black lines. This lead-tin yellow (as well as our present-day naples yellow), in combination with black, presents a particularly happy note of color.

The chair was obviously not done alla prima but was painted in two stages. First a light ocherish tone was allowed to dry on the imprimatura-covered canvas. Next a glaze of burnt sienna was brushed on the lower part. Bold accents in opaque burnt sienna can be seen underneath the sleeve and, in one spot, on the upright rail of the chair. I mention this slight detail only because there is a marked "trickle" at the edge of these passages. It appears that this overpaint did not go on very well on top of the underpainting, a condition with which every painter is familiar.

In figure 46, the painting of the gloved hand represents the ulti-mate in vigor, dash, and assuredness of touch. Here the simplicity of the technique could not possibly be carried further. The gray scumble (on the dark imprimatura) stands for the shadows; the lights were scumbled into this (wet) tone with a dozen brush strokes, and the whole was then strengthened with accents of black color dashed off with incredible gusto. I do not exaggerate in saying that the painting of the gloved hand must have taken less than fifteen minutes.

Color Section

Fig. 2A. Experimental delineations made with gum tempera into a

Fig. 3B (above) made with paint thinned with copal concentrate.

Fig. 30A (see next page). Pieter Breughel (1520?–1569). "The Harvesters."

Fig. 48A. El Greco. "The Cardinal."

8

THE SPANISH SCHOOL
EL GRECO, VELAZQUEZ, GOYA

THE THREE GREATEST Spanish names in the world of art are El
Greco (1541?-1614), Velazquez (1599-1660), and Goya (1746-1828),
and each provides us with a different approach to the technique of
oil painting. El Greco's background so far as technique is concerned
belongs to his Venetian training and the undoubted early influence
of Titian and Tintoretto. Velazquez, on the other hand, received
his greatest influence from direct contact with the Flemish master,
Rubens. Goya, working about a hundred years later, was left without the closely guarded workshop methods of the late Renaissance
and of the Dutch and Flemish schools. He was thus obliged to experiment with the oil medium to a far greater extent than his pred-
ecessors and his work thus becomes more closely allied to the work
of the modern school.

Following Italian traditions, El Greco's method of underpainting
was free enough to allow improvisations. On top of the white lead
ground, a priming in red, pink, or gray was used, a practice we still
follow today. A point of interest is afforded by Ruhemann's discovery that tempera was used under an oil glaze on one of El Greco's
small canvases. Why he should have resorted to a tempera underpainting (presumably oil tempera) is hard to understand, considering
his technique. But, since no other paintings by him seem to reveal
similar treatment, it may be assumed that this might have been in
the nature of a single experiment.

The fact that El Greco frequently retouched—evidenced by his
contemporary Pacheco's criticism that in doing so he worked "very

89

hard for poor results"—would at least prove that he did not use an "archaic" type of underpainting.

It is to be noted that in any method which calls for "retouching paintings over and over again," the reliance upon glazing must largely be abandoned, for any retouching of glazes—unless done with great circumspection—would, of course, undo them. Now, there is not much orthodox glazing to be found in El Greco's painting, with the exception of areas done with madder lake—a favorite color of his—which he used on a grisaille foundation. Whereas the early Flemish and Italian masters would carry out all the gradations of monotones meticulously and glaze them to coincide precisely with the grisaille, El Greco's underpainting as well as glazing is rough. Even the madder lake shows an impasto in some passages, a quite unconventional way of using this color.

Although there is evidence of grisaille underpainting under flesh tints in many of his paintings, again it is not the same kind of grisaille that we find in Dürer's or the Flemish work, or in some of the early Velazquez.

The dissimilarity of the surface appearance of the various works of El Greco suggests that the medium is not the same as that used by Titian, his one-time master. Whether El Greco had at his disposal stand oil (which originated in the Lowlands) cannot be answered, but that he might have thickened his linseed oil by exposing it to sunlight is likely, for such method of thermal oil processing was traditional in Italy where he received his training. However, the polymerization of the oil must have been, as a rule, slight. This can be seen from the paint conformation, which is quite different from that of Rembrandt or some of the Flemish masters.

The presence, or the absence, of a hard resin in the painting medium is another rather moot question. We know, however, that frequent overpaints in polymerized oil invite cracking of the paint film unless handled properly, whereas a resin-varnish medium permits continued overpaints. As to the conspicuous fact of an almost total lack of cracks in El Greco's paintings (except those brought about by external causes), a number of reasons are to be considered besides the possibility of his use of hard resin. First there is the matter of the canvas, which is exceptionally strong and densely woven. The solidity of the paint, which did not suffer shrinkage, is another reason; and finally the paintings were apparently left alone for centuries. Only comparatively recently has El Greco been "rediscovered," and the absence of damages such as befell more popular works may be due partly to their escape from the hands of imprudent restorers.

If we consider El Greco's colors, their chromatic pitch is such that

90

it makes us often regret to see his paintings cleaned as has been done in later years, depriving them of much of their original mellowness. For example, his "View of Toledo," in the Metropolitan Museum collection, after the cleaning it received some years ago, appears strangely cold, somewhat vacuous, and lacking in subtleness. Others of his cleaned paintings, such as the "Gethsemane" in London's National Gallery, are also distressingly changed. Instances such as these, however, do not detract, in my opinion, from El Greco's greatness, though they may bolster the theory held by some that his work has been overestimated in the current wave of his popularity.

The brightness of these newly cleaned paintings, which are done over a relatively dark ground, does away with what has been regarded as an axiom by most researchers, namely, that a light underpainting —or rather priming of the support, such as seen on Flemish panels— is generally responsible for the light appearance of oil paintings after centuries. Indeed, for many years I also accepted this as a fact. But, provided that we exclude a black or an extra-dark underpainting, and apply the colors with impasto, there is no danger that a correctly compounded oil paint will change much in time. This reversal of opinion is understandable when we examine so many of the old masters' paintings, now deprived of the yellow or brown varnish film and scum which concealed their true appearance.

However, painting onto a dark surface can also be healthy—as witness the work of Goya, who came onto the scene much later. Glazes in some of his work cease to be glazes in the true sense; they are merely thin paint passages. Thus, the characteristic scumbles found their fullest use. Now to scumble, or paint a light onto a dark color, is of course a common practice in oil painting. However, the degree of contrast, and the fact that the color on top remains semi-transparent (that is, does not become completely intermixed with the wet underlying color) makes Goya's method particularly characteristic.

Goya's painting ground was predominantly red. But as much as I tried to understand its nature without benefit of a chemical analysis, which to my knowledge has never been made, all I could think of is that the paint was not a pure iron oxide red, such as our venetian red, for it is not opaque and dull. Nor does it impress me as vermillion. He might have used a burnt ocher for example, or perhaps a mixture of white lead and an iron oxide red. In one instance at least, in the portrait of Infanta Maria Luisa, the color of the priming is typical of lead oxide.

Goya's painting medium must have varied, for in a working span of more than half a century, at a time when shop traditions were not observed, a lot of experimentation obviously went into his paintings.

91

Fig. 47.A. El Greco. (1548?–?1614). "Expulsion from the Temple" (detail).

Fig. 47B. El Greco. "Expulsion from the Temple" (detail).

Above, Fig. 49A and, opposite page, Fig. 49B. El Greco. "The Virgin with Saint Ines and Saint Tecla" (two separate details).

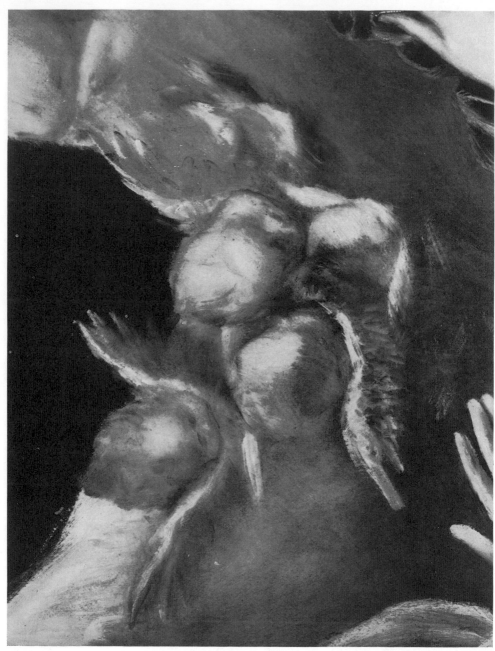

Fig. 49C. Enlarged
detail from the pre-
ceding illustration.

Fig. 48. El Greco. "The Cardinal" (detail). See also color section.

97

Velazquez, who was nearer to the time of El Greco, was certainly one of the greatest portrait painters we know. Comparatively speaking, his work was not distinguished before Rubens' arrival in Spain in 1628, but his contact with the great Flemish painter at that time gave him the opportunity of learning first hand many of the shop secrets developed by this master from the north. The assimilation of the principles of aerial perspective and the technique of producing very powerful effects with the use of a very thin paint can partly be attributed to Rubens and partly to a first-hand study of the works of the Italian masters during a sojourn in Italy. The resulting technique developed by Velazquez falls between the Italian School, exemplified by such masters as Tintoretto and Titian, on the one hand and Rubens on the other, but the individuality of the Spaniard is evident in the sharp and piercing realism of his approach. And perhaps the most interesting characteristic, from a painter's point of view, that emerges in his canvases is the ability to say so much with so little paint. In this respect he might be said to have excelled both the Italians and those of the Flemish School.

Velazquez's later work was done entirely without an underpainting, merely utilizing a toned ground or imprimatura.

We can learn more about the techniques of these three painters by following our previous method of analyzing specific examples.

El Greco. "Expulsion from the Temple" (Details), Figures 47A and 47B. "Cardinal Nino de Guevara," Figures 48 and 48A. "The Virgin with St. Inez and Saint Tecla" (Details), Figures 49A, 49B, and 49C

In El Greco's paintings the colors sparkle and glow, sometimes almost bordering on the garish in their intensity, yet they were all painted on a relatively dark gray or red ground.

In the "Expulsion" the paints must have had a fair degree of viscosity, judging from the conformation of the brush strokes and the character of the blending. Observe the painting of the coat on the man to the left of figure 47A. Here a thinly applied burnt sienna color rests on a light underpainting where it appears glowing and light, and on an opaque layer where it appears dark. On top of it the lead-tin yellow, brushed in with a few pastose strokes, serves as a high light.

Observe. the contours which run along the arms and legs of the figures. They separate the figures from the background in strong definitions. Here linear and pictorial means are combined and harmonized with great understanding. Perhaps only Tintoretto in his best work approached such problems in like manner. Similar treatment of contours—here limpid, here incisive and sinewy—are evident around the figures in the second detail shown in figure 47B.

Especially well exemplified is the brushing technique on the female figure to the right of the same illustration, where the garb and the dress are painted in less than twenty major strokes of a fuzzy, round, soft-hair brush. These brush marks seem to have been left unblended, and all the mellowness arises from the automatic fusion of the extra long lead-tin yellow painted into the wet underlying color, apparently an umber. This sketchy technique, which nevertheless appears quite finished and weighty, cannot very well be manipulated alla prima. Indeed, only a succession of overpaints can explain to us the contrived alla prima effects, so different from the "direct" alla prima work of a Frans Hals.

That the canvas is well underpainted (again as contrasted with Frans Hals's work, for example) can be realized from the fact that none of the texture of the canvas is discernible in the middle areas, which invariably receive the chief attention of the painter and where most of his elaborations occur, although the texture is clearly visible toward the edges of the painting.

With the advent of El Greco, a new freedom in the handling of oil paint was established which, from that time until our own day, has hardly been advanced. Note the impressionistic articulations of the brush in figure 48, which represents part of the tunicle of the cardinal shown in figure 48A. This nervous staccato and twist of the brush stroke can be likened in its spontaneity of movement to a rapidly jotted-down handwriting.

The lace work of the tunicle was scumbled with white (not particularly long in quality) into the thin, dark, and wet paint. This dark color is thin enough to be influenced to some extent by the color of the underpainting, which lends to it a particularly beautiful resonance. When the underlying colors are not visible, as is usually the case in El Greco's paintings, their presence can be sensed from the texture, which quite often does not coincide with the texture of the overpaint. This can be seen in the segment of the robe to the left of the lace in this same detail, where the conformation of the grisaille and the overpaint in madder lake are at odds.

An extraordinary orchestration of brush strokes is displayed in the head of the Virgin. The folds and the frills of the veil are not realistically presented, but rather they convey the feeling that the veil induces in us. Hence we can refer to El Greco's method here as well as in many other paintings as expressionistic.

In an example such as this, it becomes obvious that the character of contours accounts in large measure for the artistry of the painting.

And to achieve this intensity of feeling, a variety of underpaintings would have to precede the final painting. In other words, a certain density of paint is a prerequisite. Frans Hals's contours are also freely brushed, but there is an entirely different tension in the impasto of El Greco's contours from that felt in the alla prima "sweep" of Frans Hals's improvisations.

The importance of using different type brushes in the creation of paintings such as El Greco's is quite apparent. When with the help of a magnifying glass we study the veil of the saint in figure 49B and the group of angels in figure 49C, we see that the expressiveness of these passages rests to a great extent on the variegated textures of the surfaces.

Velazquez. "Philip IV," Figures 50 and 50A (early date). "Philip IV" (Detail), Figure 51 (later date)

The earlier portrait of Philip IV, from the Frick Collection, shown in figure 50, is almost three hundred years old, yet such details as shown in figure 50A bring to mind an impressionistic method of brushwork. Executed partly alla prima, this painting has the characteristic of a straight oil painting done on a very thin-toned ground. The handling of the brush is just as free in its impressionistic approach to details as that by El Greco.

It might seem that such a shorthand approach, circumventing, as it were, the painstaking work that a literal representation entails, is easier than a method following the principles of miniaturistic precision. This, of course, is not so. For, in an impressionistic rendition of this kind every motion of the brush must be right from the start. Hence the assuredness of touch in such technique is all important.

The technique used in the second portrait of Philip IV, from the National Gallery in London, would have been considered "modern" two centuries later. With the exception of the brocade pattern, a detail of which is shown in figure 51, and a few minor retouchings, the execution can be looked upon as alla prima. The paint shows no signs of polymerization and it is so thinly applied as to reveal the grain of the canvas throughout. The texture of the canvas was utilized to produce fuzzy brush strokes by dragging a semidry brush over the coarse fabric. Such effects are especially apparent where the brush carried a light color.

After a recent cleaning, the paint shows an extraordinary freshness and is completely free from all signs of deterioration. This cannot always be said of his earlier works employing overpaints and a more elaborate finish. Here we have an example where an alla prima technique claims, to all appearances, greater permanence.

Goya. "Doña Maria," Figures 52 and 52A. "Infanta Maria Luisa" (Detail), Figure 53. "The Bull Fight," Figures 54, 54A, and 54B "The Forge" (Details), Figures 55 and 55A. "Majas on the Balcony," Figures 56, 56A, 56B and 56C

These examples selected from Goya's work of his middle years to old age are rather dissimilar in their technique.

"Doña Maria," shown in figure 52, done when Goya was almost eighty years old, was presumably a commissioned work. It is very thinly underpainted, with no emphasis on textures or color. The brushwork shows a certain assured skill but no display of what we would classify as virtuosity and brilliance such as we admire in the "Majas on the Balcony" (figure 56).

The portrait must have been executed in two sittings with over-paints chiefly in the face. The canvas ground, as can be seen through the semitransparent and rather awkwardly brushed background, has a warm gray color. This thinly painted background does not meet the contours of the face so as to blend with it—a tedious procedure in merging a semiglaze and an impasto surface. Here the painter decided to meet the emergency with a black outline (see figure 52A). This unorthodox incident is especially worthy of notice as it points to the painter's unconcern with the niceties of a conventional paint routine—hence this technique impresses us as spontaneous, if at times rather careless. Yet, in spite of the modesty of pictorial means displayed, the authority of the master is still present. Note the treatment of the kerchief held in the gloved hand. This is scumbled vigorously with a few compelling strokes of light into the wet black color of the dress.

Evidently two kinds of brushes and a palette knife were used for this painting. The marks of the sable brush appear chiefly in the glove, the lace, and the hair. The lace around the neck was put in with fewer than ten strokes of the palette knife, which was moved in short, vertical strokes; and on the fringe the imprints of a sable brush are visible. The white paint was ground coarsely in a vehicle which must have been well polymerized. The same observation can be made on what appears to be lead-tin or a naples yellow, both of which, as we know, are even more reactive than white lead. I do not mean to say that a thermally processed oil was used here; there are no indications of this. But, as we know, all linseed-oil paint in time, when not kept in airtight tubes, becomes polymerized through oxidation. A discussion of this follows in the second part of the book.

The painting, treated largely alla prima (with the exception of the face and some other details), is perfectly free from cracks or any

101

signs of deterioration, but in a recent cleaning of the picture, I have been told, the black color proved to be fragile.

It is interesting to compare this portrait with the "Infanta Maria Luisa" (figure 53). Much softer and more classic in spirit, the "Infanta" was done some three decades earlier, at a time when Goya preferred red grounds. It can be considered a work painted entirely alla prima, for it was finished, it appears, in a matter of a very few hours.

Goya started with a surface which eliminated, de facto, most of the preliminaries. The red priming (it is really of an orange color very much suggestive of minium) provided the middle tone for the dark passages and a surface for him to model in light, and to scumble. It is utilized so skillfully that it remains largely visible throughout the entire canvas, thus unifying the tonality of the whole. The face of "Maria Luisa" is modeled in two tones: the shadows, applied transparently, merely strengthen the color of the toned ground; the lights are painted opaquely. The intermediate tone is the original toned ground slightly tinted by the colors of the merging light and shade. The essence of this short-cut method can be observed in the painting of the child. Here a pink color was lightly brushed, to define the lights, and on the arm the orange-red toned ground was left untouched to serve as the shadow. This procedure which, incidentally, must have allowed the painter to finish the likeness of the child literally in a matter of minutes, can be best compared to drawing with a light crayon on a dark paper, where the entire procedure is limited to heightening the form by use of the light color.

The entire background is painted with a warm-colored glaze of umber and black—a swift and effortless work. The great charm of the painting lies in the liquid, white scumbles of the dress which create a flickering sensation of soft light moving swiftly on the demarcations of the brush. This effect is unlike the one in the "Doña Maria" portrait, for only a chiaroscuro can really produce such a sensation of light. As we realize, the treatment of the latter work is almost in *plein-air*.

It is obvious that to be successful in alla prima painting such as is exemplified here, one must possess an unerring skill in draftsmanship.

"The Bull Fight" (figure 54) shows much the same technique as in the last portrait discussed. It, too, relies almost entirely on short cuts. In the group of spectators at the upper left of the picture there is very little variation in the brown tone of the underlying color. (This is too opaque to be called an imprimatura). On this shadowy background surface the figures were drawn in outlines, the color of the background running right through them. This, in effect, is painting in open color. Utilization of open color is also seen throughout many other details of the painting. The figures in light are also outlined, but in addition they carry coherent patterns of high lights put in with impasto—and with the bravura of a great virtuoso in chiaroscuro technique.

The shadowy masses with the dark delineations, the large area of light (lower right), and the staccato of the small light patches distributed "just where they belong" help immensely to hold the whole composition together. It is obvious that were the figures in the shade to carry individual color patches the unity of the whole would be greatly impaired.

The unconcern with which the painter dismisses the matter of details is quite remarkable. The figures on the entire arena in the background, for example, are not delineated in a draftsmanlike manner with a pointed brush. Here a fuzzy brush was used to produce broad, painterly effects. Likewise the spots of light were set in with an almost impressionistic manner. Although this painting may not have been executed in one sitting, it can be looked upon essentially as an alla prima work.

In the detail in figure 54*A* the method just described is well exemplified. On the head and shirt of the figure (which measures about six inches high in the original) the dark underpainting (or, perhaps I should say, toned ground) was left open. The light color of the arena, which serves as the background, was painted around the figures (see the demarcation of the brush next to the head of the figure at the right). The most complete freedom of handling, however, is seen in figure 54*B*. Here knife and brush were used to produce impetuous effects of light.

In contrast to the preceding paintings, "The Forge" (figure 55) is built up in a totally different manner. Here overpaints and variable textures abound. Large areas of this big canvas were painted entirely with the palette knife in bold strokes. Both the white and the dark paint are predominantly long and heaped up in impasti. The gist of the procedure is as follows: When the painter starts to paint with a dark impasto paint, a large quantity of light color is needed to counteract the dark color, hence he is compelled to employ vigorous scumbles and an aggressive brush and palette knife stroke. This is seen in the detail in figure 55*A*, in which a veritable battle of broad palette knife and brush strokes has been waged.

Although in essence this manner of painting is somewhat akin to Rembrandt's, the analogy must remain remote because of the distinct individualities of each artist. Moreover, the physical properties of Goya's paint are manifestly different.

Fig. 50. Velazquez (1599–1660). "Philip IV." Early painting.

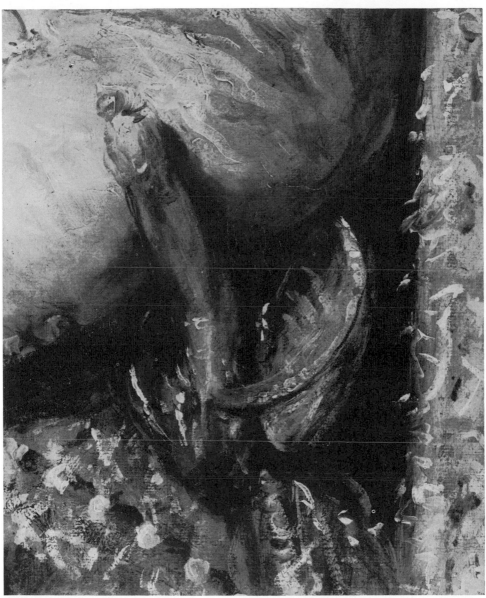

Fig. 50A. Detail of sword hilt from painting on opposite page.

Fig. 51. Velazquez. "Philip IV" (detail). Later painting.

Fig. 52. Goya (1746–1828). "Doña Maria."

Fig. 53. Goya. "Infanta Maria Luisa."

*Above: Fig. 54.
Goya. "The Bull
Fight." Right: Fig.
54A. Detail from
the same picture.
See also opposite page.*

Fig. 54B. "The Bull Fight" (detail). See also opposite page.

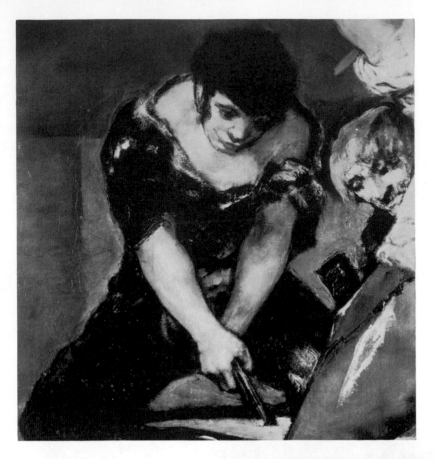

*Above: Fig. 55. Goya.
"The Forge" (detail).
Right: Fig. 55A. En-
larged detail from the
section shown above.*

*Opposite page: Fig. 56.
Goya. "Majas on the
Balcony."*

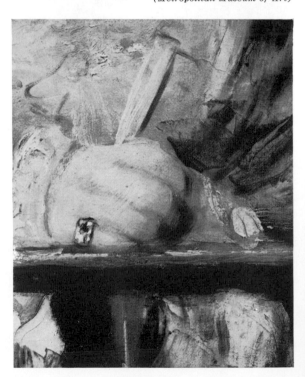

Fig. 56A, above, and Fig. 56B, right. Goya. "Majas on the Balcony" (details). See also next page.

Fig. 56C. "Majas on the Balcony" (detail from sleeve of the lady at left). See Fig. 56, page 113.

As to the precise nature of the underpaintings—for there must have been a few of them—no conclusion can be made because of the general opacity of the impasto on top. But, whatever indications are to be found, all point to an underlying paint of dark color.

In the "Majas on the Balcony" (figure 56) the painter's mastery in the use of the palette knife is perhaps more remarkable than in any other painting. The painting starts with a simple underpainting scraped so thin in some places as to reveal the white priming which covers the top grain of the finely woven canvas. This underpainting is kept in very few colors: a red (possibly burnt sienna and umber) for the background, pink under the dresses and flesh, and ocher in some places. The painting develops rather placidly, only to burst out in a veritable riot of dazzling knife strokes. (See figures 56A and 56B.)

In contrast to "The Forge," where the palette knife operates all over the canvas, in the "Majas" the knife work on the dresses, shoes, fringes, and laces offsets the enamel-like smoothness of the flesh and the thinly painted background.

To follow the master's hand as it moves on this canvas, study the photographs of the details through a strong magnifying glass. In figure 56A, for example, the knife carrying black, white, and possibly naples yellow progressed swiftly in short strokes, diagonally along the sleeve, the paint being mixed directly on the canvas. The marks represent the pattern of the brocade and the frills at the edge of the sleeve. The brocade of the bodice carries also the marks of the knife, though the instrument was held here flatly and not edgewise toward the canvas.

In figure 56B the shawl was painted with very few, large, sweeping strokes of the knife, to which, here and there, an accent of the brush has been added. In these passages the freedom in the handling of the brush and the knife is complete, but it stands in sharp contrast to the treatment of the flesh and the background with the shadowy figures which are smooth in texture and conventional in technique.

In figure 56C, representing the sleeve at the shoulder of the figure on the left, delightful impressionistic effects were produced by a combination of brush and knife work.

116

9

EIGHTEENTH- TO NINETEENTH-CENTURY ROMANTIC PAINTING

I HAVE GROUPED in this chapter four representative painters who, although quite different in point of technique, broadly speaking show a certain kinship of spirit. They are all of the Romantic School and belong to centuries far removed from the great patronage of the church. Along with the other equally famous artists of their time, they struggled to find wealthy patrons of another sort. Of course Magnasco and Gainsborough are different, not only in the fact that the latter was primarily a portrait painter, but also in volatility of spirit, so to speak, which gives them a radically different approach to romanticism. It is perhaps the nervous mechanism of the artist's hand that would impel a Magnasco to slash out with a brush, a Guardi to improvise in staccato, and a Gainsborough to practice reticence and restraint, especially when engaged in his fashionable portrait work. As to Eugene Delacroix (1798-1863), the leading Romantic of the nineteenth century, he combined the ideas of Rubens with the Victorians' spirit at its earliest inception.

Alessandro Magnasco (1667?-1749). Italian. "The Baptism of Christ" (Detail), Figure 57

Magnasco, as we have it from contemporary reports, was another painter capable of dashing off a canvas such as the "Baptism" (which measures nearly four by five feet) in a matter of hours. The swiftness of his technique may thus parallel that of Tintoretto, Rubens,

117

or Hals, yet his style differs as much from the work of any of these masters as their styles do from one another. As an artist he is also of lesser stature.

To produce an instantaneous sensation of flickering light, the use of a dark ground appears to be a prime condition for creating contrasts (see figure 57). By the painter's leaving much of the canvas steeped in gloom, the staccato effect of the eerie light conjures up moods of mystery or enchantment. Yet the darkness in such an ensemble does not create the impression of a vacuum; on the contrary, it stimulates the imagination and adds greatly to the drama of the scene. This is a tricky kind of technique, because so much of the effect relies on the response of the observer's emotions. We can see that this eclectic painter borrowed much from the physical and esthetic characteristics apparent in the work of the earlier Venetian, Tintoretto. Yet Tintoretto, more sure of his genius, could afford to be even more daring in certain respects. Thus we have an interesting comparison, which has had so many parallels throughout the history of art, of a younger or later painter borrowing certain effects from a great master and concentrating on or exaggerating one particular aspect or mood. We call such an approach "mannerism."

Francesco Guardi (1712-1793). Italian. "A Seaport and Classic Ruins in Italy" (Detail), Figure 58. "The Rialto," Figures 59 and 59A

In the "Seaport" painting Guardi has effected a theatrical illumination. The light, as it were, is cast from a narrow focus and travels from the extreme side and strikes the contours of the objects on its way. Like the light of the rising and setting sun, it produces an effect of chiaroscuro. In such a light-and-shade relation there is little space left for tonal transitions, for the starkness of contrast is of the essence in achieving dramatic emphasis.

In "The Rialto" (figure 59), Guardi employed an entirely different method, one that depends largely on graphic effects. It is only natural that a draftsman of great proficiency, such as Guardi, would exploit delineation even in his paintings. And so the nervous line peculiar to the late Baroque manner and the low-focus light are the mainstay of his art. However, the calligraphic ideas are not entirely his own; they were employed in the work of Giovanni Battista Tiepolo, whence they came to Guardi when the latter was almost fifty years of age.

Now we have referred to "filling in" a drawing with color, as was the manner of the archaic painters, and we have spoken of "painting with color," as we see it in El Greco and others. In Guardi's "Rialto" both the painterly and graphic means are combined, although they act independently. The delineations are superimposed on top of the "finished" painting for the sake of an illustrative effect.

Thus the house in the detail shown in figure 59A was first finished in color, and the definitions of masonry were done on top of the dry paint surface with black, crisp lines. These lines, in my opinion, were very likely done with a pen rather than with a brush, or possibly with a combination of both. The systematic exploitation of the pen in oil painting is to be observed in the work of Canaletto (1697-1768), who may have been the originator. If used before in many other oil paintings, I have failed to recognize it as such.

In the type of work represented by Guardi and Canaletto, a pen can produce a flat line of uniform thickness more easily than can a brush and thus is effective in defining architectural details. When a pen is used, one must avoid the use of a polymerized or resinous medium and paint must not be thinned with turpentine because such media inhibit the free flow of paint. Pure unprocessed linseed oil is best for this purpose.

The surface upon which such delineations are done should not be too slick or it may cause the paint to trickle. To avoid this and make the paint behave, brush turpentine onto the paint surface and leave it to evaporate before any pen drawing is attempted. Another way to condition a surface for receiving fine lines is to rub chalk onto the paint film with one's finger. If a little chalk is left on the surface, the edges of the lines will appear rather soft.

If India ink is used for the delineation instead of oil paint, it is well to treat the paint surface carefully with much-diluted ammonia instead of turpentine.

Guardi's underpainting was, as a rule, held in middle tones. Chiefly pink, gray, and brown were used on broad areas without any modeling. The fine lines—other than those done by the pen—were painted with a brush which we would now call "No. 1 extra-long sable."

Gainsborough (1727-1788). English. "The Painter's Daughter Mary" (Detail), Figure 60. "Miss Margaret" (Detail), Figure 61. "Mrs. Elliott" (Detail), Figure 62

In a technique that calls for a delicate, smooth, and easy touch, heavy impasti, overpaints, and bold brush strokes are more or less impossible except, sometimes, in the treatment of accessories. Here the painter's brush need not always be quite so well behaved as, for instance, when flattering a model's features.

Fig. 57. Alessandro Magnasco (1667?–1749). "The Baptism of Christ" (detail).

Fig. 58. Francesco Guardi (1712–1793). "A Seaport and Classic Ruins in Italy" (detail).

Opposite page: Fig. 59.
Guardi. "The Rialto."
See also detail, below.

Fig. 59A. Detail from Guardi's painting on opposite page.

Fig. 60. Thomas Gainsborough (1727–1788). "The Painter's Daughter, Mary" (detail).

Fig. 61. Gainsborough. "Miss Margaret" (detail).

Fig. 62. Gainsborough. "Mrs. Elliott" (detail).

Fig. 63. Eugene Delacroix (1799–1863). "Abduction of Rebecca" (detail).

The romantic portrait of Gainsborough's daughter in figure 60 has a porcelain delicacy and refinement. We note first that the texture of the canvas is conspicuous for its silky fineness. Upon a sand-colored priming which left very little tooth on it, a brownish glaze was applied in a rather uneven, spotty fashion to enliven the appearance of the background. This glaze, strengthened a little here and there with darker tones of the same color, makes up the shade of the face. The same color is again used in the area of the hair and the modeling of the ear. Wherever soft outlines appear, they utilize the fine texture of the canvas. This technique produces an effect somewhat akin to a drawing made with charcoal on paper, where the charcoal merely marks the fine tooth of the paper, and the undergrain remains untouched throughout. How different the contour created by this technique is from the one seen in Goya's Doña Maria (figure 52). In Goya's painting there is a measure of boldness and freedom, in Gainsborough's a carefully followed routine.

In the painting of the flesh, first a light and thin grisaille must have been applied, presumably into the wet glaze which covered the entire canvas. The thin painting of the flesh could hardly have been an alla prima work on the rather dark surface, for delicate nuances are much easier to produce on an existing foundation of a light grisaille. Indeed, such an initial grisaille would allow the painter to finish the work in one short sitting.

In the detail in figure 61 representing another portrait of the artist's daughter Miss Margaret as a young woman, the technique is reduced to the simplest pictorial means. Only great skill could render the structure of an eye, for example, so effortlessly. Scarcely ten delicate brush strokes can be counted here, yet they tell the whole story.

In the portrait of Mrs. Elliott (figure 62), the simplified formula of a successful and fully employed portrait painter can be seen. Without trying to minimize Gainsborough's extraordinary craftsmanship, we nevertheless see in this portrait, as in others, a pervading air of carefree facility which borders on fashionable superficiality. Elegance is the underlying theme. As John Ruskin aptly said, "Gainsborough's hand is as light as the sweep of a cloud, as swift as the flash of a sunbeam."

Observe the treatment of the hair on this portrait which, except for the few limpid, thin glazes, shows some fluffy strokes of a semidry brush, a whitish-gray scumble. The few darker accents are painted as thinly as in water colors. All this was done on a brownish middle tone which amounts to nothing but the priming of the canvas.

The face might have been underpainted in a very light grisaille; or, judging from its enamel-like and radiant quality, it could simply have had a white color underneath, over which the delicate tones

128

were brushed lightly—so lightly, in fact, that the fleeting strokes of the pointed, fine sable brush hardly touched the face except here and there on the eyebrows, eyelashes, nostrils, and mouth. There is something almost Oriental in the character of these brush marks, which suggest calligraphy, but the figure and the landscape are treated wholly in a broad painterly manner.

Eugene Delacroix (1798-1863). French. "Abduction of Rebecca" (Detail), Figure 63

In some paintings Delacroix might almost appear to have outdone Rubens. There is even a copy he made of a Rubens painting which hangs opposite the original by the Flemish master in the Royal Museum in Brussels. In many respects this is more spirited in technique and of greater interest pictorially. Generally speaking, however, although this great French painter aspired to the heights of Rubens and earlier masters such as Tintoretto, it is doubtful whether he reached their heights. This may be due partly to the materials he used, partly to the romantic approach popular with painters in his time, but it is due also to that indefinable attribute, genius, which, although often present, did not reach a comparable greatness. Often his figures take on something of the quality of a cardboard cutout rather than full-blooded people. In the "Abduction of Rebecca," which is a fairly good example of his manner, he made use of a varied imprimatura (burnt sienna, ocher, viridian, ultramarine) which handsomely permeates the tonality of the whole picture, but he fell short in the impasti and was lacking in the seemingly casual verve that distinguishes the work of Rubens. His daring was more self-conscious, and the air of moderation observed in the use of brush strokes, contours, and textures fails to complement the Baroque in concept and design. Herein, I believe, lies his lack of vitality and his weakness of presentation.

Although, as a painter, I am partial to impasti and associate them with "strength," I must try to qualify this preference, although it must not be forgotten that strength can also be rendered by linear means. As to the latter, no free delineations, or, perhaps I should say, emphasis created by the use of an outline exists; the background meets the contour in a realistic, not a pictorial, manner. And, as regards impasti, consider, for example, the ring on Rebecca's finger and the four buttons embellishing the cuffs of the abductor's helper (aside from similar trivia placed elsewhere), would an impasto technique allow the execution of this clutter of nonessential knickknacks? Hardly; they would lose themselves in a maze of the paint matter.

PART II

Present-Day Materials and Techniques
for Master Craftsmanship

10

PAINTING MEDIA
THEIR PROPERTIES AND USES

SINCE THE EARLIEST DAYS of oil painting, raw linseed oil (and, more rarely, heat-processed oil) has been used for grinding pigments. Although modern, factory-produced paint is also ground in raw linseed oil, it nevertheless differs radically from that of the old masters'.

Yet the difference between the materials employed by one or another of the old masters was often quite marked. The difference to which I refer rests in the nature of the oil medium which serves to thin the paint and which is responsible for the characteristic of the paint body. Of course, the nature of the stabilizer and the characteristic of the pigment itself—that is, the size and shape of its particles —will also produce a paint material specific as to its consistency and viscosity. (For stabilizers see page 170).

As to the binder, or the vehicle as we call it (and I refer here only to linseed oil), it can be neutral or it can contain free acid (in various degrees); it can also be polymerized to a lesser or greater extent.

Modern Tube Paint

Modern tube paint is prepared with raw, unpolymerized oil. This accounts for the crisp, short quality of the paint body. As we mentioned, the term "short" refers to a paint which, when heaped up or manipulated with the brush, retains its sharp conformation. "Long" paint, on the other hand, flows more easily and tends to seek the level; thus it does not hold brush marks well, or at least its brush marks are round-edged and soft in appearance. Such brush marks are observable in the paintings of the early Flemish and Dutch masters, among others.

In addition to the presence of aluminum stearate, the fact that modern paint is encased in airtight tubes and thus does not undergo polymerization aids in preserving its quality of shortness. Consequently modern tube paint produces brush marks which are hard-edged. Moreover, such paint is deficient in regard to blending. When manipulated with the brush, commercial paint does not fuse in the manner of paint prepared with polymerized oil. All this leads us to the conclusion that, when we change the viscosity of tube paints, their behavior will at once be altered.

Older Types of Paint—with an Oil Binder

Linseed oil, when in contact with air, develops free acid and becomes polymerized to a lesser or greater degree, depending on the duration of the exposure. In many of the old masters' paintings, the appearance of the paint conformation clearly points to the use of polymerized oil. It may also be noted, in relation to this, that prior to the advent of collapsible tubes paints were not kept in airtight containers. Consequently, some polymerization of the oil must have taken place because of its contact with air, and with this action the paint body changed from a short to a longer condition. This is one reason that older paintings, more often than not, show different surface characteristics from modern ones, a difference that can be seen in many illustrations of old masters' paintings introduced in the preceding chapters.

Stand-Oil Paint

Pigments ground in stand oil or sun-thickened oil are much tougher than paints ground in raw oil, but the excessive viscosity of such paint does not always serve the artist's purpose. However, viscosity can be regulated if the heavier oil is added (in amounts varying according to the degree of viscosity desired) to paint which has first been ground in raw oil. It has also been found that a light-bodied, sun-thickened oil that has been exposed to oxidation for a short period of time may very well be used for the grinding of some paints. Moreover, the painting medium itself, if prepared from a polymerized oil, will impart greater toughness to the paint.

Resin-Oil Paint

Aside from differences due to the basic nature of the vehicle, the introduction of resin into paint also changes the quality of its body. Resin can enter the paint in a volatile or an oil solution (that is, dissolved in a solvent such as turpentine or oil). Because high temperatures are required to melt resin into oil, maximum viscosity can be produced in such compounds. Neither resin-in-turpentine nor resin-in-oil can very well be added to paint which is to be stored in tubes because some pigments react with resin and harden or become "livered." This is attributed to the high acid value of the resin. However, resin may be added to the paint placed on the palette prior to painting, as we shall see later.

Pigment-Oil Relation in Tube Paints

The amount as well as the quality of the oil in which pigments are ground contributes to the consistency and viscosity of paint. In the best quality of modern tube paints, only as much oil as is needed to produce a dense, brushable paste is compounded with the pigments. When a manufacturer advertises his product as containing the maximum of pigment and the minimum of oil, he implies that he is giving the artist the best value—but this does not necessarily mean that such paint is desirable under all conditions.

It must be understood that the lasting quality of paint depends to a great extent upon the ability of the binder to hold the pigment particles together. However, since the tendency of oil (unprocessed linseed oil, at any rate) to yellow and darken has been observed, some writers on technique stress the necessity for using a minimum of oil. While it is true that an excess of even the best purified linseed oil is undesirable, it is also true that an insufficient quantity of the binder can impair the stability of paint very seriously.

Proper Bond of the Pigment Particles

Commercial tube paints may not contain an amount of oil sufficient to give them maximum permanence. This means that, once dry, some colors in time have a tendency to rub off, if the painting is cleaned, for example; and with progressive age their film will undoubtedly weaken. Hence the belief that it is best to use paints just as they come from the tube is usually incorrect. Indeed, it is safer to err in the direction of an excessive use of a good binder than not to use enough. However, because not all pigments solidify equally well with the admixture of oil, some require the addition of polymerized oil. There is also a danger that the oil may shift to the lower layers while drying and leave the top layer of paint without a sufficient bond.

135

Painting Medium as Supplementary Binder

The term "painting medium" refers to any of a variety of diluents used for thinning present-day tube paints. Modern, machine-prepared tube paint is denser in consistency than paint composed of hand-ground pigments, for mechanical grinding permits the use of far less oil than is necessary in grinding pigments by hand.

The commonest of the paint diluents and the one especially favored by the generation of painters preceding our own is turpentine. (How well I remember the aroma that permeated the studios of my teachers, early in the century!) Turpentine is sometimes used for diluting paint directly and sometimes added, in greater or smaller amounts, to the oil. In the first case, unless used sparingly, turpentine will unavoidably weaken the cohesion of the paint film and thus cause its early deterioration. In practice, a correct proportion of turpentine can be managed only if mixed directly on the palette with a certain quantity of paint, for if one dips the brush into the turpentine cup at random and then mixes it with paint, the turpentine dilution will become disproportionately large. When turpentine is mixed with linseed oil in the cup and then used for painting, the oil film will be thinned and thus its resistance to abrasion and weathering is reduced.

Raw Linseed Oil as a Painting Medium

There is nothing one could justifiably say against the excellent properties of linseed oil as a binder for pigments. It is the best of all the drying oils. Yet, it has decided drawbacks as a painting medium, inasmuch as it limits the painter's technique. Linseed oil cannot very well be used with the profusion required when glazing or scumbling, as yellowing and often wrinkling would result; in any case, the physical properties of the material are not quite suitable for this purpose. Moreover, frequent overpaintings on a surface saturated with a fatty medium should be avoided if one wishes to insure the permanence of a painting. Therefore, when using pure linseed oil, one should refrain as much as possible from overpainting, and work rather alla prima.

The drawbacks of raw linseed oil as a painting medium may be listed as follows:

1. Lack of sufficient viscosity, hence poor faculty for blending paints. Because of low viscosity, superimposition of paint layers while painting wet-in-wet is not feasible.

2. Although the adhesive properties of linseed oil are excellent, it lacks what we may call, for want of a better term, the capacity to

"stay put." Therefore, when used abundantly, it will run down on a vertically placed canvas.

3. Unsuitability or limited usability for glazing and scumbling.

4. Unsuitability for use in frequent overpainting.

5. It lacks sufficient body to provide the requisite bond for certain pigments, which do not solidify well in it.

Thermally Processed Linseed Oils as Painting Media

After having used these media, both sun-thickened linseed oil and stand oil, for a long time, I have come to believe that the latter is preferable, even though the former too is excellent.

As regards resistance to moisture and dirt, the linoxyn of stand oil is superior by far to that of unprocessed linseed oil. It is thicker and also tougher, hence less likely to suffer damage from handling or cleaning at a later date. When used as a painting medium, stand oil limits the painter's technique as much as the raw oil, except that it does not incline to yellow to any marked extent. The working qualities of stand oil as a painting medium are somewhat improved if it is mixed with turpentine.

Let us summarize briefly the salient qualities of stand oil. Although its excessive use is not otherwise objectionable, like unprocessed linseed oil it lacks the capacity to "stay put." It, too, if applied as a liquid, will run down the surface of the canvas before it has the opportunity to dry. The greater viscosity of the oil will allow scumbling and glazing, but with the same hazard, that of its sliding down the canvas (see figure 64, page 220). Furthermore, overpaintings on top of a surface saturated with stand oil will, because of excessive slickness, become even more difficult.

The Role of Resin in a Painting Medium

The answer to the problems listed in the preceding paragraphs is the addition of resin to the painting medium. This creates a condition in which paint manipulations otherwise difficult or impossible immediately become feasible.

The advantages of using a resinous medium cannot be impressed upon the painter too strongly. They are: (1) Increased brilliance of colors and capacity to fuse. (2) Added viscosity, which permits a more varied manipulation of paint (that is, the execution of glazes and scumbles and certain kinds of impasti). (3) Ease of overpainting onto wet and semiwet surfaces. (4) The increased bond between the priming and the paint stratum, as well as between the various paint strata. (5) The possibility of a substantial dilution of the oil with a

137

volatile solvent such as turpentine, thus in effect reducing the content of oil in the medium. This permits increased use of the medium with the paints, without corresponding increase of the "fatty" content. (6) The faster drying quality of paints mixed with a resinous medium (especially when copal resin is added).

The Presence of Hard Resin in Old Masters' Paintings

This has always been a controversial subject, since written records and literary accounts concerning it are equivocal. However, reasonable conclusions can be reached if we consider certain facts.

Let us assume that we have made a painting, employing for this purpose a brush fully loaded with a liquid, stand-oil compounded paint. Having done so, we should have to place the canvas in a horizontal position very soon after the paint had been applied, for otherwise it would run down the surface, or at least move from its original position, leaving droplike marks or runs. Paint of equally liquid consistency which has had a resin added does not have this tendency to run downward (see page 220). It seems only reasonable to assume that a hard resin was used in the paintings of some of the old masters which unmistakably show the conformation of a heavy liquid paint, and in which no evidence of a run is seen. I say specifically "a hard resin," for all experienced researchers agree that in those paintings showing extraordinary toughness of the paint film the presence of a soft resin must be excluded.

The Presence of Soft Resin in the Paint Body

By means of microchemical analysis Dr. Coremans, in Brussels, has established the presence of a substance in the painting medium of many old masters which has characteristics similar to those of some natural soft resins. While chemical analysis does not, in a positive fashion, show the presence of a resin, the absence of a soft resin in a paint film may be established by its resistance to the action of certain solvents. For example, a well-aged linoxyn does not yield to the action of alcohol, whereas the paint film dissolves readily, regardless of its age, if it contains mastic (soft) resin, which is soluble in alcohol. To be sure, a small quantity of a soft resin may not produce such a drastic effect, but the amount that is generally recommended and used today would invariably affect the stability of the paint. If the paint film contains damar (soft) resin, it is susceptible to the action of such a relatively mild solvent as toluol or xylol. Acetone, however, one of the strongest solvents known, is not an entirely efficient

138

solvent for resin, dissolving damar, for example, only to the extent of 70 per cent.

Soft Resin Deficiency

Exactly when soft resin first appeared as part of the painting medium cannot be determined with certainty, but its use was already widespread among nineteenth-century painters. At the present stage of our knowledge of painting materials, the use of a soft resin seems unwise, although a great many contemporary painters still employ it.

My own experience provides an example to illustrate this point. In the process of cleaning, it was recently necessary to remove the old varnish from some of my paintings done in the early 1920's. The paintings were done with a medium the formula for which had been worked out by my one-time teacher, Max Doerner. It contained a relatively large proportion of mastic (soft resin). There were some glazes on the paintings made with burnt sienna and viridian green and some rather thinly executed passages of ocher, ultramarine, and black. Although I used a very mild cleaning agent (mineral spirits and some xylol), after a few minutes of gentle rubbing with a piece of absorbent cotton the glazes started to come off rapidly; then the thin paint applications became affected; only impasti, especially those produced with white lead, at first held relatively well. After prolonged rubbing, however, even the impasti showed an inherent weakness due to the presence of soft resin.

Hard Resin

I assume that the reader is acquainted with damar and mastic, the soft resins. However, knowledge as to the nature and behavior of the hard, or fossil, resins, as they are called, seems to be very scant even among the better-informed writers on paint techniques.

Hard resins are found underground, being exudates from coniferous trees now extinct, whereas the soft resins are products of freshly tapped, living trees. The term "hard resin" as generally used, however, is not quite specific, for many border cases are often classified as hard; and among themselves the hard resins vary not only in chemical composition but in certain qualities they exhibit, such as degree of hardness, purity, and color. True hard resin may be recognized by the fact that it does not soften in boiling water in the manner of soft resins and will not dissolve in any known solvent without previous thermal processing.

"Congo copal" is a general term applied to a certain kind of resin found in the Belgian Congo, the quality of which varies in purity, color, and degree of hardness. The higher grades of the resin are lighter in color and contain less foreign matter, while the finest grade is clear as glass and is totally free from impurities. Both its freedom from impurities and the lightness of its color influence the final color of the melt, but it is doubtful whether these qualities affect the permanence of the material or its tendency to darken. It is safe to say that a varnish prepared even from the darkest run will not become darker than its original color; on the contrary, when exposed to light, some bleaching will occur.

Mention should be made here of a hard resin known as Zanzibar copal which possesses a characteristic "gooseflesh" surface. This particular copal is quite useful in spite of its dark color, for its hardness exceeds that of all other grades. Greater hardness, of course, requires higher temperatures for processing.

Thermal Processing of Congo Copal

Copal resin in its natural state cannot be completely dissolved even in the most powerful solvent we possess. However, it softens to a gel and dissolves partially in tetrachlorethane, butyl alcohol, and diacetone alcohol. It is then possible, by a process of distilling, to obtain in liquid form part of the resin which has been dissolved. This may be combined with turpentine or linseed oil, for example, and an almost colorless copal preparation is thus obtained. However, such a material does not suffice for our purposes. We need *all* the constituents of copal, and its total solubility can be obtained only by subjecting it to high temperatures, liquefying it by the application of heat, and keeping it heated for a length of time sufficient to make it compatible (that is, soluble) with oil as well as a volatile solvent. This processing of the resin is referred to as "running."

The running of hard resins was first mentioned in the manuscript book of Theophilius, written in the twelfth century. Theophilius, it appears, had already made a distinction between hard and soft resins. He described the incorporation of soft as well as hard resin in oil, and the method of preparation he set forth remains essentially unchanged to our day. Here is Theophilius' account of the preparation of hard resin, quoted in full:

"Place together four stones which may be able to sustain the fire without flying to pieces, and place a common pot upon them, and put into it the above-mentioned gum fornis, which in Romaic is called *glassa,* and upon the mouth of this pot place a smaller pot, which has a small hole in the bottom, and lute a paste around it, so that no vapour may come out between these pots. Then place fire carefully underneath, until this gum liquefies. You will also have a thin iron rod fitted to a handle, with which you will stir this gum, and with which you can feel when it is quite liquid. Have also a third pot nigh, placed upon the coals, in which is hot linseed oil, and when the gum is quite liquid, so that the iron being extracted a kind of threat is drawn out with it, pour the hot oil into it and stir it with the iron, and thus cook them together that they boil not violently, and at times draw out the iron and daub a little over a piece of wood or stone, to try its substance. And take care in this, that in weight there are two parts of oil and the third part of gum. And when you have carefully cooked it to your wish, remove it from the fire and, uncovering it, allow it to cool."

Although in the past I have also repeatedly advised the painter to add Copal Concentrate, which is an oil varnish, to his paints. I do not claim that this advice originated with me. It was, in fact, Theophilius who said, *"First grind your colors in liquid oil, then before painting, mix three [that is, a few] drops of the varnish with your paints."*

The Technique of Copal Running

The lumps of resin (not less than a pound in all) should be broken up to about the size of hazelnuts, that is, about half-inch cubes, by crushing them in a brass mortar. They are then placed in a pot of aluminum or stainless steel. Iron or copper vessels should not be used, for they considerably darken the color of the melt. Having the resin lumps of the correct size is important in the process of running, since too great heat would be needed to melt large chunks of the resin, and if it is reduced to dust or too small particles, the resin will fuse too rapidly and its liquefaction will be impaired. The equipment used for the running of resin in commercial manufacture is rather elaborate. However, the painter needs but a small amount of the material, a half pound of run copal being enough for a year's work. Therefore he can dispense with most of the paraphernalia, even with the thermometer which, in a commercial plant, is of prime importance, since temperature governs the entire running process. Control of the whole operation is much simpler, however, in running a small quantity.

It takes a temperature close to 600° F. to liquefy the resin. To make resin compatible with oil a somewhat higher temperature is

141

necessary, while to dissolve it in mineral spirits a prolonged cooking at about 650° F. must be carried out.

It is safe to say that under ordinary circumstances a painter will not wish to go to the trouble and expense of scientifically controlled thermal processing; as a matter of fact, he does not need to do so. All he need do is to fill a suitable vessel half full of crushed resin and place it over the flame of a Bunsen burner. It liquefies, depending on the quality of the resin, in about one hour of heating. When the lumps start to disintegrate, the resin should be stirred constantly until all the solid particles liquefy, when it will drip from the stirring rod like a hot oil. At this point, the flame of the burner should be turned down to prevent the melt from foaming and boiling over. It should be mentioned that the operation involves considerable fire hazard in the hands of an inexperienced person!

If the resin is to be incorporated with linseed oil, heating can be discontinued upon liquefaction of the run. If it is to be dissolved with mineral spirits, prolonged cooking, about thirty minutes or so after the liquid state has been reached, should be carried out.

The melt should be poured while still liquid into a shallow aluminum or tin pan and allowed to cool. After it has cooled, the dark brittle mass can simply be knocked out of the pan and crushed to small particles and powder in a mortar. This is easily done, for the lumps are quite brittle. In this form it is ready to be used in the preparation of varnishes or painting media.

Incorporation of the Run Resin in Oil and Volatile Solvents

After the run copal is crushed to powder, it should be placed in a bag made of cheesecloth or any other porous, lint-free material and submerged in turpentine or mineral spirits, where it will dissolve readily.

To incorporate run resin with oil, it is necessary to subject it to further thermal treatment. Stand oil is more suitable than raw linseed oil for this purpose. The oil should be placed in an aluminum container or a beaker and the powdered resin added to the oil. About 10 per cent resin in the mixture will suffice to give the painting medium the desirable quality.

The oil and the resin should be heated to about 450° F. over the flame of a Bunsen burner or on an electric plate. This temperature should be maintained for about ten minutes, and then a test should be made by dropping a small amount of the mixture from the stirring rod (which, by the way, should be of metal or glass) onto a glass plate. If the resin has not been well enough assimilated with the oil, the drop will look turbid upon cooling. One should continue cook-

142

ing the mixture and repeat the test until the test drop cools perfectly clear. This operation should be accomplished in about fifteen minutes. It is common studio practice to judge that the requisite temperature has been reached when the resin dust that settles at the bottom of the vessel fuses into the oil. Thereafter the same degree of heat should be maintained. If an electric plate is used, the switch may be turned at regular intervals from high to low to keep the required temperature constant.

The longer the compound is subjected to heat, the more viscous it becomes. To store the medium in a jar, one should pour it while still hot, as lower temperatures greatly inhibit the flow of the liquid.

The Difference Between Copal and Damar Resins as Part of the Medium

As far as actual behavior under the brush is concerned, that is, in practical application, the difference between copal and damar resin in the medium is not marked. However, even before the painting is done, the painter will discover that the copal product sets more quickly and firmly and that this permits a more efficient manipulation while painting wet-in-wet. An even more important difference is that damar resin loses its cohesion and disintegrates in time, whereas copal, because of partial polymerization, becomes more resistant with age. In other words, certain molecular changes take place in copal resin which contribute to its stability. This does not mean that even an aged copal-oil film will not yield to a strong solvent, but it can be said with certainty that its resistance to any kind of solvent will be incomparably stronger than that of a medium containing a soft resin.

Tests of Copal and Damar Preparations

The following tests were carried out by Mr. Charles Ferri, research chemist with the American Gum Importers Laboratories.

The compounds tested were:

(1a) Copal Concentrate (copal—stand oil: equal parts, the first by weight, the second by volume)
(1b) Damar concentrate (damar—stand oil: same solution as above)
(2a) Copal Varnish (a 15 per cent solution in mineral spirits)
(2b) Damar varnish (standard solution, that is, about 25 per cent in turpentine)

143

(*3a*) Copal Painting Medium (a 15 per cent solution in stand oil, linseed oil, and turpentine)

(*3b*) Damar Painting Medium (same solution as above)

First, each of these compounds was flowed onto a tin panel and permitted to dry for a week, then immersed for six hours in mineral spirits. The results were as follows:

(*1a*) Unaffected

(*2a, 3a*) Slightly softened

(*1b, 2b, 3b*) Considerably softened and partially dissolved

A test for resistance to moisture was made in which samples of the subject compounds were immersed in cold water for forty-eight hours. The results were as follows:

(*1a, 1b*) No marked changes

(*2a*) Less affected than *2b*

(*3a*) Little change, far superior to *3b*

A test for resistance to boiling water, each compound being immersed for fifteen minutes, produced the following:

1. Change in hardness:
    (*1a, 1b*) No marked change
    (*2a, 2b*) Induced brittleness
    (*3a, 3b*) Softened
2. Change in color:
    (*2a, 2b, 3b*) Turned white
    (*1a, 1b, 3a*) Turned brown-yellow
3. Color recovery:
    Damar preparations remained white. Copal preparations recovered partially.

The following tests were made by myself for color of the various films.

The compounds tested were:

(*a*) Linseed oil

(*b*) Linseed oil with excessive amounts of cobalt dryer

(*c*) Stand oil

(*d*) Copal Painting Medium

(*e*) Copal Concentrate

(*f*) Damar Painting Medium (stand-oil compound)

(*g*) Damar Painting Medium (linseed-oil compound)

(*h*) A 5 per cent amber-oil solution of a foreign make

144

All these preparations were painted on glass slides, then left for a period of time in darkness exposed to atmospheric humidity of 45 to 80 per cent. At the end of eight months they were compared to fresh, dried films and they showed the following characteristics:

(*a*) Considerable yellowing and slight wrinkling
(*b*) Excessive wrinkling, deep brown-yellow color
(*c, d, e, f*) Slight yellowing
(*g*) Considerable yellowing
(*h*) Considerable yellowing and wrinkling

They were held in darkness after this for a total period of four years. During the remainder of the four-year period the condition of yellowing did not increase further.

At the end of the period, all samples were exposed to strong daylight and, for intermittent periods to sunlight, but the colors of the films did not improve. The same compounds were mixed with white-lead oil color and exposed for a year to the conditions described above. The yellowing of the original white colors corresponded to that of the pure oil films, but when exposed to strong light, all samples bleached out, though not in the same measure, to show satisfactory whiteness.

As regards elasticity of film, a 50 per cent solution of copal and stand oil was permitted to dry out to a thickness of $\frac{1}{16}$ inch. After ten years the sample still possessed elasticity not unlike that of fresh rubber.

Tests for drying:

Samples of oil paints prepared with copal resin dried materially faster than pure oil paint samples, and the solidification of paint progressed quickly throughout the entire thickness of the film.

The following tests were made to investigate cracking of paint films:

An application of light ocher (which is a relatively soft paint) thinned with Copal Painting Medium was allowed to dry on a tin plate for a week. One sample then received a coating of a 30 per cent solution of copal in mineral spirits (an excessively strong concentration), and another sample a coating of a 50 per cent concentration of copal in stand oil. After seven years' time, the two samples were examined under a magnification of ten times actual size. No cracks at all could be observed.

Conclusions in Regard to Copal Media

1. In all mixtures with oil colors, especially when used for glazing and scumbling, a Copal Painting Medium because of its resistance to solvents, must be rated above the standard damar formulas used today, which have unfortunately proved to be perishable.

2. The very slight yellowing found in paint compounded with the copal media which was kept some time in darkness, does not exceed that of the best grade of stand oil, the least yellowing of all the forms of linseed oil. The cause of yellowing must be sought in the inherent nature of linseed oil and not in any tendency of copal resin to change color with time.

3. Copal has not been observed or proved to cause cracking of any kind when used in a painting medium or in a varnish. Assertions made by certain authors to this effect have never been substantiated.

Historical Evidence and Controversy

Often enough, very contradictory statements, some praising and some condemning the use of copal resin are found. In support of its high value, I should like to quote from various sources.

A. P. Laurie, in *Materials of the Painter's Craft,* says: "It has not been sufficiently realized that the lowering of tone of oil pictures is largely due to the collection of dust on the porous surface of the oil. We have here, therefore, another argument in favor of a highly resinous medium . . . In fact it might be suggested that the perfect preservation of pictures at certain periods may have been due to the accidental use of copal resin for varnish-making."

Prof. A. H. Church claims that "when copal is incorporated with a certain proportion of oil, it forms a surface which is hard but does not crack, and which is preferable to oil alone, which is soft."

It has further been brought out by Sir Charles L. Eastlake that the Flemish painters prepared a medium by dissolving amber in oil, and mixed a little of this resin-oil with paints which had first been ground in pure linseed oil. He states that such a medium protects the pigments from moisture and deterioration.

As stated earlier in the book, there is evidence, according to Dr. Coremans, that hard as well as soft resins were imported into Flanders even before the time of van Eyck, and it is entirely possible that copal from the Congo was widely available. It should be remembered that the most precious and widely used pigment of the Middle Ages, lapis lazuli, was a far more exotic importation than copal would have been, and infinitely more difficult to procure. Rutherford J. Gettens, in *Alumni,* 1950, XIX, pages 3-4, writes: "The only source of supply of this precious stuff in past centuries was in the mines located two days' journey from Iskasar, at Ser-i-sang, in the upper Kokcha valley between Parwara and Lower Robat, Badakhshan." We might add that, up to the present date, only a few white

146

men are known to have reached this precise geographic location in Hindu Kush. However, to get copal, it was not necessary to go even as far afield as to Africa, for it is reasonable to assume that amber, which has always been found in abundant quantities along the Baltic coast and which is also obtainable in many other localities in Europe, must have been used in painting. We have ample documentary evidence that amber served as a varnish in antiquity. In fact, the word "vernice" at one time meant amber. For all practical purposes, amber, which is also a fossil resin of a coniferous tree, may be considered to be identical with copal. Today, however, copal is in much better supply than amber, and can be obtained in a quality superior to that of amber.

As to the supposed darkening of copal, here the foremost authority on the technology of resins, Dr. C. L. Mantell, Director of Research of the Netherlands Indies Laboratories, author of many important scientific papers and co-author of the book *The Technology of Natural Resins,* by Mantell, Kopf, Curtis, and Rogers, a five-hundred-page volume, states: "Copal film does not darken, but it actually bleaches upon exposure." It is worthy of remark that those contemporary authors who do not approve of copal happen to have had no practical experience with it, and are not familiar at first hand with its formulas and preparation. This is clear when one studies the text and wording of these writers' statements. It is perhaps amazing, but it is a fact that the first comprehensive description of the material and its preparation ever to have appeared in an art manual can be found in one of my own books published ten years ago. No one, it seems, had undertaken up to then to investigate the over-all aspect of the problem from the viewpoint of the painter and to publish a treatment of it in detail backed by practical experience.

Industrial Copal Preparations

Accurate data concerning the practical use of copal preparations is available from the beginning of the nineteenth century. At that time the product was used for industrial purposes, chiefly for varnishing objects exposed to weathering. It also became a favorite varnish for making the old masters' paintings look *really* old, a simple method quite in keeping with the taste of the time. Such industrial varnish was prepared from the commonest grade of copal, incorporated in linseed oil without regard to its quality. To promote quick drying, it was saturated with manganese or lead dryers, and as such it found its way into the artist's studio. As we know, it is the dryer that imparts undue hardness to a paint film and promotes

147

brittleness and excessive yellowing. Hence, when used as a painting medium, such a compound would surely cause serious damage to the paint body. When applied as a varnish to relatively fresh paint, its removal would hardly be possible, for it would incorporate itself permanently into the paint stratum. As an "old master" varnish, fortunately, it does not seem to have caused any damage, for today, after the removal of the varnish, we can clearly see the excellent state of preservation of many of the old masters' works. We might even say that the old, inferior industrial varnishes apparently were quite beneficial in protecting these paintings.

Copal Formulas

In my own formulas for copal preparations, which are now manufactured commercially by the Permanent Pigments Company, of Cincinnati, Ohio, I have endeavored to be guided by certain logical considerations: (1) The medium should not call for a manner of procedure different from that which we are accustomed to give any ordinary paint thinner. (2) It should allow the widest variety of technique, from painting in the thinnest fashion, in the manner of water color, to extreme impasto. (3) It should possess the requisite viscosity. (4) It should dry within a day or two. (5) It should permit frequent overpainting. (6) It should possess a minimum amount of resin and linseed oil.

The formulations which have these qualities are known as Copal Painting Medium Light and Copal Painting Medium Heavy. They differ from each other merely in degree of viscosity. However, they differ considerably from all the other copal formulas on the market both in the quality of the resin and in working qualities.

Copal Concentrate

This compound produces an oil color comparable to that seen on early Flemish paintings. The Concentrate is a thick, viscous, honey-like substance, combining copal and stand oil. The painter should mix it with every color as it comes from the tube, using as much of the Concentrate as desired, and employing a palette knife in the mixing.

The Concentrate, according to the amount added, conditions paints so that they all become long, flowing, and more lustrous. Flake white is the only exception to this rule; since it is a highly reactive paint, because of saponification by the oil content. A small addition of the Concentrate to it makes it rather stiff (due to formation of lead soaps), and hence more suitable for use in heavy impasti.

148

A larger addition of the Concentrate causes the paint to become long.

The less a pigment is capable of solidifying the admixture of oil, the more it improves with the addition of the Concentrate. I refer here to colors such as ivory black, alizarin crimson, barium yellow, and strontium yellow. All the earth colors become more viscous and stringy. Some others, such as naples yellow and vermilion, become semiliquid when mixed even with a small amount of the Concentrate. However, the addition of the Concentrate causes all of them to develop a much thicker linoxyn than they otherwise would.

A paint prepared in this fashion should be used for the final painting, but *not in the underpainting*, for it forms an exceedingly tough, nonporous film. Thus it possesses maximum resistance to dirt and the action of solvents in future cleaning. However, should overpainting of a paint stratum containing Copal Concentrate be desired, it is advisable first to treat the surface with fine sandpaper and then brush some turpentine on it. This will insure better adhesion of subsequent paint applications and eliminate trickling.

Concerning the Old Masters' Media

It is obvious that the difference between the techniques at the command of certain old masters within any period, and certainly within any century, must have been considerable, although we know that, during periods when shop traditions prevailed, painters were in a better position to learn handed-down procedures. Rubens' methods were quite different from those of Botticelli, and Rembrandt's means were unlike those of Raphael. The Flemish paintings from the fifteenth and the first part of the sixteenth centuries have a different paint conformation and different characteristics of execution from the paintings of, let us say, the Venetians of the Titian-Tintoretto age. As to permanence, it is conceded by experts that the Flemish work is unsurpassed. It is also accepted that linseed oil alone could not produce the surface characteristics found in these paintings. Stand oil could do it, but only if mixed with paint to a very firm consistency; as soon as a more liquid condition of the paint is attained, the wet film has a tendency to slide down on the canvas to some degree.

Summary: Painting Media

Modern paint differs from that of the old masters in point of viscosity; tube paint is, as a rule, short.

Stand oil and resin varnish added to paint change consistency.

149

It is better to use too much of a good binder than too little, if one must err in one direction or the other.

Turpentine and turpentine-oil mixtures are unsatisfactory diluents. Thermally processed oil is excellent, but has certain disadvantages.

Soft-resin oil compounds fail to give permanence to paints.

The composition of the old masters' painting media is no longer a "secret." Hard resin compounds were known and prepared early in the history of painting. Conclusive tests prove the superiority of copal media.

11

UNDERPAINTING AND OVERPAINTING

The Alla Prima Method

THE FEW GREAT WORKS of art painted alla prima may be said, in general, to fall into two categories represented respectively by the work of Frans Hals on the one hand and that of Pieter Breughel the Elder on the other.

Frans Hals' mastery, as we found in discussing his work in the first part of the book, lay in the unparalleled virtuosity of his brush. Measured by the highest standards, many of his paintings show an inherent weakness, not in any lack of technique, but rather in the quality of his perception. I have in mind some of those dashing performances which, as compared with Rembrandt's deep, laborious work, built up as a rule of many paint layers, impress us at times as somewhat superficial. If we endeavor to rationalize this condition from the viewpoint of technique, we might perhaps conclude that Hals' speed of execution did not, as a rule, permit the painter to penetrate the surface of his subject nor to build up the subtle inner qualities which distinguish a work by Rembrandt. We must grant that a one-operation painting is limited in regard to the use of variable textures such as high impasti and also glazing and scumbling. As we know, glazes can have only a very narrow range in alla prima technique, but the recognition of this fact is far from implying that an alla prima method always narrows the painter's articulation. It merely differs, because of the simplicity of the means employed, from the more complicated procedure which relies on frequent overpaintings.

The second category of alla prima painting, best represented in the work of Brueghel, is quite different. Here the painting was finished alla prima on an imprimatura foundation and, except for occasional corrections, which appear sometimes in several superimposed paint layers, there was no systematic overpainting. The greatness of these paintings lies not in any intrinsic paint quality, but in their spiritual depth, their imaginative content, and their extraordinary manner of composition. Brueghel's way of painting has none of the bravura found in all prima works by Velazquez or Rubens, none of the flashes of passionate temperament of a Frans Hals, yet his restrained technique is of the highest eloquence.

We are similarly able to speak only in general terms of more complicated techniques that involve a variety of underpaintings, which I shall describe briefly in this chapter.

Repeated Overpainting

Paintings which are purposely built up on a succession of paint layers have certain remarkable characteristics. They seem to breathe out an energy which emanates, as it were, from the very stratification of the paint layers. It is as though the painter's incessant return to the charge created an atmosphere of persuasiveness which at once communicates the painter's vision.

A concrete example from my own experience comes to mind. A painting of a head was done in one operation directly on a toned ground (in this case, a light gray color applied on top of the original white priming). Then I started to change it, and overpainted the canvas from one corner to another. By continuing to overpaint the sum total produced a dense web of color and texture which was radically different from the appearance of the initial painting. The remarkable fact in such a procedure is that, although all apparent traces of the various stages of the painting may have disappeared, nevertheless the hidden layers of paint continue in some mysterious way to aid the final effect of the painting. Even though the final

151

overpainting may actually be accomplished in a matter of minutes, the painting will appear "finished," for the final speedy rendering is backed by much labor, search, and accumulated effort; hence, through a process of evolution, it may attain particular depth and expressiveness.

Overpaints and Permanence

It is my experience that the presence of a resinous content in the medium permits numerous overpaintings without harming the body of the paint. On the other hand, the liberal use of linseed oil as a diluent for the paint, which is always required to produce glazes and scumbles, will not permit successive overpaintings without the risk of future deterioration. More often than not, the presence of over-painting contributes nothing to a painting's permanence; quite the contrary if the overpainting has been executed in a manner disregarding the principles that govern the achievement of permanence. It is in the very nature of the creative process that, during its moments of most intense accomplishment, the mere pedantic observation of methodical procedures is hardly uppermost in the mind and sometimes goes completely out of the window. Therefore it would seem that alla prima painting may often have a better chance of physical durability over the centuries.

The Priming

White lead, as we know, is the leanest of all oil paints. This is only one of several reasons why it is the only material suitable for priming the (glue-sized) canvas. The paint used for priming, usually two or three coats, which must then carry all the overpaints, should be thinned a little with copal varnish. A leaner and a more absorbent priming will thus be obtained, and the addition of the resin will also accelerate the drying of paint. To speed up the drying even more, some umber or manganese blue oil color can be added. A perfectly white ground will rarely, if ever, be required. Priming should always be done with the palette knife, and the layer (or layers) of paint should be scraped on as thinly as possible.

Toned Grounds

Direct painting on a white-primed canvas or panel was not practiced before the time of the Impressionists. An imprimatura or a colored priming, more or less uniform in tone, invariably covered the white ground except in the work of the Primitives.

My experience has led me to doubt whether a white priming is of value when using overpaints. The one-time belief in the importance of a brilliant white priming for the preservation of luminosity does not seem to be substantiated by the appearance of many of the old masters' paintings which have now been cleaned.

Red, gray, yellow, and brown grounds were used by the Renaissance masters; such priming was also popular with many painters of the nineteenth century and just before, including Goya, Degas, Delacroix, Courbet. Wooden panels of the early painters carried a white gesso ground often toned with an imprimatura.

Red Ground

It cannot be said summarily that a dark ground always causes the lowering of a painting's tonality. This is true in many cases where a thin paint film was used, notably in the work of Titian, Tintoretto, and especially some French Pre-Impressionists. That it does not always apply is shown in the work of Goya, who painted almost exclusively on such a ground, which is especially adapted to a technique that relies largely on scumbling, a favored device of this master. To be sure, we should also take into account the fact that Titian's work antecedes Goya's by more than three centuries.

On many occasions I have studied Goya's red priming, and although I cannot say whether he used vermilion, ocher, or an iron oxide red with or without white lead, it appears that the red coat was in many instances scraped over a light priming with a palette knife so thinly as to permit the light ground to show through the superimposed red color. Thus Goya's red grounds retained, quite often, a good measure of reflecting power.

Vermilion requires but little oil and, as it produces a lean paint, is the most suitable red for priming. In itself, of course, it possesses great luminosity. Since it forms a somewhat horny surface in drying, it is necessary when using it as a priming coat to sandpaper it smooth before proceeding with the painting.

As compared to a neutral-toned ground, however, red priming poses some problems in regard to the general coordination of the color scheme, especially in subject matter other than portraits and figure studies.

Yellow Grounds

Although yellow might seem a color to be avoided in an underpainting, on the ground that it might contribute to a general yel-

153

lowing of the colors, such a supposition is unfounded. The kind of yellowing that is produced by inferior oil or an inferior white pigment is different in nature, and produces a different effect from what we might call a yellow "inner light." As a matter of fact, a yellowish color, in the form of an imprimatura, was favored by the Flemish masters and is found in the panels of some of the early painters as well as in paintings by Rubens. Yellow was frequently used as a solid underpainting beneath the green areas of the seventeenth and eighteenth century landscapists, and has even been used under skies, as witness paintings by Turner. I consider that a strongly tinted yellow priming contributes greatly and even imparts a kind of radiance to thinly applied dull or dark-color passages.

However, if one wishes to follow the principle of painting "fat" on "lean," it is not advisable to use cadmium yellows for this purpose. White lead, as always, should be the body color, and cadmium or hansa yellow can then be used as the coloring matter. Hansa yellow is rich in oil, to be sure, but a very small amount of this permanent aniline color suffices to give a strong tint to the white. This procedure is entirely in keeping with the old masters' practice of tinting white lead with a yellow lake or pigment. Of course, all the yellow earth and mars colors can be used, mixed with white, when a more brilliant toned ground is desired.

Neutral Grounds

Neutral colors can best be likened to pastel shades, for they are all drained of chromatic strength. By virtue of their neutrality, these colors are naturally correlated and can be interchanged almost at will. Variations of grays, greens, and pinks are used, as well as a pale, ocher tone which can also be considered as neutral. The principal color is in every case white lead. At its side we place umber and prussian blue, for grays; the same combination, plus ocher, for greens; and white lead with venetian red for pinks.

The question arises as to why we should resort to an indefinite color, such as a neutral priming, in preference to an underpainting in varied colors. The reason is that the use of neutral tones for priming often obviates the need for underpainting. In portrait painting this is certainly the case. A skilled painter should be able to emulate, in speed, if not in artistry, Gainsborough, Goya, Frans Hals, and others, who were all able to finish a head in one sitting. Since a properly chosen gray ground can very well be likened to the tonality of a grisaille, the progress of work on such a surface should be unhampered. Moreover, any underpainting desired, whatever the specific colors, can be executed on a neutral-toned ground.

As to preferring one color over another for the painting ground, the choice is, of course, a matter of personal taste. As a rule, it is more effective to use contrasting colors: that is, warm colors over a foundation kept in a cool tonality, and vice versa. However, this is not to be considered as an invariable principle. Warm colors may be overpainted on a warm base and cold on cold if desired.

The Application of a Toned Ground

Thus far I have referred to a *white priming*. A question now arises as to whether a white priming is altogether necessary. My own experience leads me to believe it is not and that we can start with a light, toned ground applied directly to the sized canvas equally well.

For the priming (or the toned ground) it is best to use a tube flake-white (white lead) or a white-lead paste such as is sold in cans (this is the more economical), thinned to a rather loose consistency with Copal Varnish. To produce a toned ground, colors should be added to the white lead without thinning, just as they come from the tube.

If a little umber is added to the white paint used for priming, the ground will, as a rule, dry overnight. The second toned ground can then be applied the next day, which means as soon as the paint is dry to the touch. There is no need to wait for a thorough drying, for the two applications will dry out together. Before commencing the actual painting, however, it is a good practice to permit the undercoats to solidify well.

If the interstices between the threads in the weave of the fabric are not well filled in with paint after receiving the two initial white-lead primings, which may well be the case if one's canvas is coarse, a third priming coat may be applied.

A knife should always be used in the application of the various paint coats. The knife blade, unlike the bristles of a brush, forces the paint into the small openings and crevices of the canvas, and scrapes the layer of paint thin where it rests on top of the thread thus producing a level surface. For unhampered work and a proper textural appearance of the finished painting, such a treatment of the toned ground I consider essential.

Imprimatura

Before discussing the problem of underpainting, let us consider its simplest form, the imprimatura. Imprimatura consists of an oil paint of any desirable color (with the exception, of course, of white) diluted with Copal Varnish to the consistency of water color. It is always of great transparency. It can be applied to a white ground, a toned ground, or any kind of underpainting, at any stage. The only condition is that the underlying paint must be dry, or at least dry to the touch, before receiving the imprimatura.

Imprimatura serves to enhance the appearance of the surface color upon which the painting is done. To be effective, the imprimatura should be employed on top of a relatively smooth ground. A canvas with too much tooth or a coarse texture is inappropriate. Applied over the smooth priming of a panel, an imprimatura treatment is most agreeable.

As I have mentioned, only Copal Varnish should be used for diluting oil colors. Whenever I mentioned Copal Varnish, I must, to avoid confusion, refer specifically to the product compounded after my own formula by Permanent Pigments. Since, in general, there is no standardization in various preparations of the resin, they cannot be used interchangeably for the purposes described. When mixed with this varnish, colors dry out rapidly and in two or three days become solid enough to be overpainted. As we shall see later, the paint surface should be moistened with the medium before painting. However, since our medium contains turpentine, a fresh imprimatura would dissolve. But, when properly dried, a copal-varnish imprimatura does not easily yield to the action of turpentine. Unlike this, a color thinned with damar varnish will always remain susceptible to the dissolving action of even a mild volatile solvent.

A Copal-Varnish imprimatura becomes dry to the touch a few minutes after its application. When immediate overpainting is desired, this can be done by using a medium prepared from Copal Concentrate in a proportion of one part Copal Concentrate to three parts linseed oil.

The imprimatura can be applied to the painting ground with a brush, a knife, or a cheesecloth, depending on the textural effects that one wishes to produce.

First Underpainting

The paint used for underpainting (consisting chiefly of a stiff white lead) should also be thinned with a little Copal Varnish. Since the liquid part of the varnish is volatile, the only deposit left in the paint will be the resin; at the same time the underpainting will become leaner and somewhat more absorbent. Since white lead paint, as I have mentioned, dominates all the other colors in quantity, there is no need to add varnish to the rest of the colors. It is important to keep the paint which has been diluted with the varnish

156

heaped up and not spread all over the palette, so as to prevent the volatile diluent from evaporating. It is not advisable to keep the varnish in the oil cup and to dip the brush into it for diluting the paint while painting, for this would cause the paint to become too sticky (because of the rapid evaporation of the diluent) to be managed with the brush.

Heavy impasti, however, should not be made in a paint thinned with varnish, because such paint, being poor in oil, lacks the requisite elasticity. Therefore, instead of Copal Varnish, some Copal Painting Medium should be added, so as to make the heavy impasti more elastic. The small quantity of oil which Copal Painting Medium possesses will not make the paint unduly "fat" for underpainting, considering the fact that such paint is made up chiefly of white lead.

It should be noted that a small addition of the Copal Medium, (and especially of Copal Varnish) stiffens white-lead paint at once. If Copal Varnish is used, the paint applied to the canvas becomes so stiff within an hour that it is difficult to move it with the brush. In two or three hours the paint becomes quite solid—but not dry.

Color in the First Underpainting

The preliminary painting should be kept in dull monotones, for there will be enough opportunity to use colors, in subsequent underpaintings.

The following colors, besides white lead, are all that will be needed for the first underpainting if more than one underpainting is contemplated: umber for dull brownish grays; venetian red for pinks; umber and prussian blue for grays; umber, prussian blue, and ocher for greenish tones; and ocher for yellows. Because of their exceptional siccative qualities, umber and prussian blue are always especially desirable in underpainting.

Strong Colors in the Underpainting

Colors such as cadmiums, burnt sienna, and the iron-oxide reds are rich in oil. Therefore, if these colors are used full strength in underpainting, they should be applied very thinly and diluted with a little Copal Varnish. As we know, any strong color can be diluted to the consistency of watercolor with the varnish and used as an imprimatura on top of an underpainting.

Second and Subsequent Underpaintings

The second underpainting should be applied directly to the first;

157

oiling with the painting medium is not required between these two layers of paint.

The function of the second underpainting is both to enrich the color and to create impasti and textural variations. If colors of stronger tints are required, the relative quantity of white lead will be reduced, and hence the paint will become richer in oil content. As I have said before, heavier impasti should always receive a small addition of Copal Painting Medium, which makes them more elastic.

Third, fourth, or even fifth underpaintings can have only one purpose—to create considerable impasti for textural emphasis on certain parts of the painting. The problem of producing such impasti has to do not only with the paint itself but with the choice of the tools as well, always considering the importance of creating a sufficient bond between the superimposed paint layers.

Impasto Effects in Underpainting

As we have already noted, both the white-lead priming and the toned ground should be applied with the palette knife. The underpainting also should be done with the palette knife, except in cases where the canvas does not have sufficient tooth and would become too smooth if treated in this manner. (Such a smooth canvas would, of course, be best suited for imprimatura.) To make sure that the interstices of a fabric have been well filled with paint, it is a good idea to turn the canvas toward the light in such a way as to reflect the glare, which will show up any inadequately filled places.

In figure 65 (top),* the grain of the canvas is too rough and the interstices are not sufficiently filled with paint. In figure 65 (bottom) the canvas was covered with paint by using the palette knife in very much the same manner as one butters a slice of bread. This technique produces a relatively smooth surface, much smoother, in fact, than any application with a brush, no matter how delicate its hair.

Figure 66 (top, left)* shows a surface on which an elastic knife was pressed and lifted repeatedly from a thick, wet paint layer, thus producing a "stippled" effect. A considerable increase of impasto can be produced when the same manipulation is repeated on top of the dry (stippled) layers. This stippling has, however, a rather mechanical appearance; its texture is materially enhanced if one brushes lightly over the wet paint with a soft-hair blender see figure 66 (top, right).*

Other variations of paint textures are demonstrated in the lower examples in figure 66.* The lower left example shows the result of the use of a bristle brush and short paint which created rather deep

See pages 220 and 221.

158

grooves. Such deep brush strokes should, of course, be well considered, in accordance with the textures planned for a painting. Haphazard, pastose brush strokes, when overpainted, are more often than not disturbing to the eye. An undesirable rough paint texture should be smoothed with sandpaper before overpainting.

In figure 66 (bottom, right) the layer of paint was applied with a palette knife over a heavy impasto underpainting (done with the brush) so as to fill the grooves created by the brush. In this manner various optical (and textural) effects can be created, especially when using contrasting colors for the two coats.

Of the paints which are most suitable for the execution of impasti, white lead, as I have said, is the first choice. For dark-colored impasti, paints such as mars black and mars brown are, because of their coarse texture and relative leanness, very suitable. (I am referring here rather to an impasto in the final painting that can be produced in one operation, for in underpainting, any number of thin paint layers can be applied in succession to produce a high relief.)

If especially coarse textures must be achieved in a painting, substances such as sand, coarse clay, pumice, crushed egg shells, and similar inert material can be mixed with the paint.

Ultimately, however, the manner in which impasti are produced is a problem of personal ingenuity. The suggestions given in this chapter are intended to indicate a direction in which the student can pursue his own search, rather than to prescribe specific formulas.

Because of its importance, let me stress the point that *in underpainting the medium should not be rubbed into the surface.* Unlike overpaintings, underpaintings should be done on a dry surface, as the object is to create a lean surface on which to carry out the final painting.

Drying Time before Overpainting

An overpainting on a freshly dried paint film will inevitably go dull. Dullness of the surface indicates a loss of oil by absorption into the lower layers; therefore, a longer wait in order to allow the various underpaintings to dry well is indicated.

Let us assume that the underpainting has dried and that one is about to start the final painting—perhaps we should say, instead, painting in full colors, for it can hardly be determined at this stage what will turn out to be the final painting. What we expect will be the "final" painting may prove unsatisfactory. In this instance, one need not wait for a thorough drying of the paint, but can continue painting from day to day. This is true because, when the painting medium is rubbed into the paint surface—our customary procedure before commencing to *overpaint*—it facilitates the incorporation of the fresh paint layers. Only a varnish-oil medium, of course, is capable of bringing about this incorporation, and this is because of the presence of resin and its volatile diluent which is part of the medium. Thus, when using the resinous vehicle and when painting *thinly,* one can continue painting from day to day. However, if one permits a few days to elapse and then considers further overpainting, it is advisable to let the various paint strata dry well (that is, for a week, two weeks, or more) before applying another paint layer.

When using impasti, painting from one day to another is not feasible; this is true because, although the film on top may appear solid, underneath the paint remains soft. Pastose paint layers should be allowed to dry throughout. Their drying, depending on the thickness of the paint layer and other contributory circumstances connected with the drying of paint, may take a week or several weeks' time. To ascertain whether the paint has dried throughout, a fingernail may be pressed into the surface. Any consequent indentation in the body of the paint indicates the presence of wet paint underneath.

Tools for Underpainting and the Appearance of Paint on the Canvas' Surface

On a canvas which has a coarser tooth, underpainting should be executed either with the palette knife alone, or first with the brush and then with the knife. The use of the knife on a rough canvas materially improves the appearance of textures in the final painting. On extra-smooth fabrics the knife cannot very well be used, for it then creates an unpleasantly slick surface. On such fabrics, a bristle brush should be employed first, followed by use of a sable brush or a soft-hair blender, to smooth out the harsh demarcations left by the bristles. If a knife is used for underpainting on this kind of fabric, the too-smooth surface thus produced can be roughened with a soft-hair blender.

The condition of smoothness or roughness of the support is also important if we consider that the surface stress of a paint layer can be responsible for its cracking. A heavy impasto applied on an overly smooth surface is apt to crack. Also, paints applied to a toothless surface may not adhere sufficiently well.

Concluding Observations on the Problems of Underpainting

Thus far I have discussed the physical aspects of underpainting.

160

The establishing of textures (studied variations in the surface appearance of paint) and the creating of color areas in the underpainting which will aid us if glazing and scumbling have been considered. I have also noted that certain schools of painting did not employ underpainting, but worked alla prima.

Rubens in his most characteristic work—generally small panels done without the collaboration of assistants—can be considered the classic virtuoso of alla prima technique, inasmuch as his original painting ground (covered with the imprimatura) remains to a large extent unobstructed. It is obvious from this fact that a different kind of draftsmanship must have gone into these paintings, a draftsmanship that did not require corrective measures. For surely, the more changes made from the original concept, the less the intrinsic alla prima character of a painting, unless corrections are made while painting wet-in-wet. Work done in this manner requires a fixed plan and does not allow much latitude for indecision. Even more important, such work should always retain a quality of sketchiness in its execution. Of course, it is perfectly possible to go on with overpaints over an alla prima painting, thus changing its character in part or in whole, and still preserving sketchiness, but this type of sketchiness will be of a different nature.

Since the first underpainting, as a rule, obliterates to some extent the preliminary drawing which was made (in turpentine-diluted color) on the primed canvas. it is necessary to revamp this drawing after each consecutive underpainting. And as the original design is likely to undergo many changes and improvements during the course of the painting, it is wise not to limit the different color areas of the underpainting to sharply defined borders, but to have each color appear to melt into the neighboring one. In other words, each color should gradually blend into the next color area before it loses its identity, as the neighboring color gains in strength and finally attains its own intrinsic value.

Not only does this treatment of color areas permit latitude in changing the design, but it also greatly facilitates the treatment of contours and contributes to their final appearance. Indeed, nothing would be more confining here than hard-edged contours, which would make the use of transparent or semitransparent color applications on top of them impossible. To be sure, the use of glazes may not be desired, and, as we know, a heavy coat of paint will cover up any mistake. Nevertheless, it is a good principle to leave oneself open to all possibilities, and to create a condition in the underpainting which would be favorable to the widest possible latitude of technical treatment.

Another important advantage, quite aside from color and texture,

161

in taking one's time over repeated underpainting before finishing the painting is that it allows the maturing of the concept. Such a procedure does not impede spontaneity, but on the contrary permits the final realization to come through with greater ease and directness.

In discussing the progress of underpainting and the development of the design connected with it, I have had in mind the use of a color which confines itself to more or less neutral tones except in paintings where a high chromatic pitch is required or cases where glazing effects in brilliant hues are to be carried out.

All this, it is easy to see, presupposes a most orderly procedure and should insure long life to a painting thus carried out. The difficulty of following the rules really starts, however, when a painting once considered finished is seen to require extensive (or even total) revision. In this case, our unsuccessful "finished" painting will become nothing else than an underpainting. The proper technique to follow here—proper, that is, if one wishes to safeguard a painting's permanence—is described in the following section on "Corrective Paint Layers."

Suffice it to say that, in addition to technical considerations, there are those of pure artistry. The technique to which I allude here aims at the attainment of color and textural intensity, such as cannot very well be produced in an alla prima fashion.

To demonstrate this point, I should like to compare the topography of paintings alternatively, by Raphael and El Greco. In Raphael's paintings, the overpaintings followed a strictly preconceived scheme which allowed little opportunity for improvisation. This is not so in the work by El Greco, whose freedom in matters of technique is perhaps more akin to our own than that of any other Renaissance painter. Pacheco, the painter who was Velazquez' father-in-law and who knew El Greco, had this to say: "Who would believe, for instance, that El Greco took his paintings in hand many times, retouching them over and over again, in order to give them those cruel alla prima strokes feigning valor." I think everyone would now agree that El Greco was aiming to liberate his painting from the bondage of "finish" and thus return it to a state of sketchiness.

Corrective Paint Layers

However much we have endeavored to carry out all phases of our painting in an orderly, systematic fashion, as if we believed that every effect could be precalculated and every conceivable move of the brush determined in advance, we may find that our aim has not been achieved. Only too often, changes, rectifications, and the retracting of initial commitments arise to plague the painter.

Therefore, if a painting has been finished and still does not satisfy our craving for perfection, we should not follow our first impulse, which invariably is to start "slapping" paint onto the canvas to cover up the mistakes, since by so doing the deterioration of the painting is assured.

When correcting a painting which at one time has been looked upon as "finished," interference of old textures with the new ones are common. Moreover, when painting thinly, one should always be aware of the possibility that, in time to come, pentimenti may appear. (A pentimento is the appearance of an underlying painting through the top layer of paint, due to the loss of opacity of the top paint layer with progressive age.)

To avoid a later appearance of pentimenti, any underlying dark color or design, if not heavily overpainted, should be erased. If the area to be overpainted in light colors is very dark, a heavy coat of light-colored paint (which will serve as a new underpainting) should be applied on top of it before commencing the final painting.

The adhesion of another coat of paint cannot be perfect when painting on such oil-saturated grounds and slick oversmooth surfaces as glazes and scumbles provide. This oversmoothness, however, may be remedied in three steps. First, the surface of the paint should be sandpapered to remove the oil film from it; second, turpentine should be brushed liberally over the surface further to "etch" it and to prevent trickling; and lastly, the surface should be coated with Copal Varnish to safeguard the new bond.

Strong impasti—that is, ridges and knots of paint—should first be removed with the scraper (a knife specially designed for this purpose) and then sandpapered down sufficiently so as not to interfere with the overpaint. The surface should then be covered with Copal Varnish. This last operation also increases the viscosity of the superimposed paint. Should such viscosity appear undesirable, "etching" with turpentine alone will also improve the adhesion and eliminate trickling.

Before overpainting a finished painting which carries layers of relatively fresh paint that cannot very well be scraped off, it is best to permit a thorough drying of the paint strata. This may take several weeks, or even longer, depending on the thickness of the paint and the nature of the colors.

Underpainting: Summary

White lead is the principal color used in underpainting. Dilute

163

white lead with a little Copal Varnish when underpainting thinly. For heavy impasti, add a little Copal Painting Medium.

Use monotones in the main. If full-strength colors are needed, apply them thinly and dilute with Copal Varnish, or use a straight imprimatura.

Do not oil the surface between the various underpaintings.

Impasti can be created with a palette knife or brush.

Allow the impasto underpainting to dry well before overpainting.

For underpainting, use the palette knife on rough primings; the brush on oversmooth primings. Always provide a tooth for the subsequent painting.

Blend the contours of all color areas thoroughly.

Before overpainting, eliminate undesirable impasti.

To avoid trickling of paint (or medium), brush turpentine onto the surface and let evaporate. An application of Copal Varnish will improve the bond still further, but painting on top of it will increase the viscosity of paint considerably.

12

OPACITY AND TRANSPARENCY
OF PAINTS

THE OPACITY of paint is always relative, for none of our lighter colors, including white lead, is entirely opaque. The only exception is titanium white, which (with reasonable impasto) is entirely opaque. Even a dense light color will appear to be only semiopaque when applied in a thin film. Most of the dark colors, especially the mars variety, can be considered opaque; even in a thin film they will effectively obscure the underlying color.

White-lead paint, although it possesses good covering capacity, after a long period of time tends to become more transparent because of its saponification through linseed oil. Consequently, every other color eventually loses its opacity to some degree when mixed with white lead. With all paints, however, it is the thickness of the paint film that ultimately decides its condition of transparency or opacity.

Transparency of paint can be produced in two different ways, by glazing and by scumbling. For glazes, one must always provide a light underpainting, whereas scumbling employs a light on top of a dark color in a semi-transparent manner. The emphasis in most of my technical writings has been on the transparency which results from painting on a light ground, for in my early days I had not discovered all the possibilities of the technique of scumbling. A technique which emphasizes glazing does not, of course, permit many

165

overpaintings. Overpaints lead to opacity, and hence it is here that scumbling proves of great value for relieving the dullness resulting from the use of dark, opaque passages.

Glazes

The appearance of a glaze is conditioned to a very large degree, as we know, by the underlying color and texture of the support. Because glazes have, as a rule, no texture of their own, they reveal and sometimes even overemphasize the textural character of the support, the underpainting, or both. (However, if a glaze shows the imprint of a brush, we may refer to a "texture" in spite of its flatness.)

In figure 67A* a glaze was applied directly on top of a white priming. The texture of the hand-prepared canvas is apparent in this example. In figure 67B* the glaze was spread onto a commercially primed canvas. The mechanical appearance of the resulting texture makes the use of the glaze on such a support undesirable.

Colors for Glazing

There is hardly any need to mention special colors in connection with glazing, for any color (except white, of course) when sufficiently diluted with the medium can be used for this purpose. The only difference between the typical glazing colors, which are transparent by nature, and opaque colors is that the former cannot be used for impasto, whereas opaque paints are suitable for pastose as well as for painting in glazes. We can also say that, on the whole (with the exception of the cadmiums), the transparent colors are also more brilliant. I have in mind prussian blue, viridian green, alizarin crimson, and in particular the relatively new and powerful monastral green and blue. Of the opaque colors, burnt sienna may be looked upon as an exception, for it possesses a particularly glowing hue when diluted to the consistency of a glaze.

Glazes are usually applied to a dry underpainting or a finished painting. It is better to paint the glazes in as soon as the paint film solidifies, so as to permit the glaze to incorporate itself and to become an integral part of the paint film proper. One should keep in mind that glazes are the first to suffer in the cleaning of paintings.

Lastly, it should be mentioned that glazing can be carried out with a bristle brush, with a flat or round sable brush, with the finger, or with a knife. The knife produces the thinnest film and brings out

See page 222.

the topography of the underpainting in full detail in a manner quite different from the brush.

Underpainting for Glazing

Thus far we have referred to the color of the glaze. However, since this color is influenced and often totally altered by the underpainting, it is necessary to give particular attention to the color of the underpainting. It is also quite important in the underpainting to provide contours that will permit the delicate glaze to combine with the impasto. The blending of a glaze and a pastose film is not feasible, for the first will always be repelled by the second, which will not yield its heavy contour.

The blending of surfaces that are to receive glazes, as well as receive opaque passages, must be carried out completely in the underpainting proper, and thus the color transition of the underpainting mediates between the final glaze and the final neighboring opaque color.

Color for the Underpainting to Be Glazed

Depending on the color of the glaze and the effect desired, the color of the underpainting may range from white to a quite dark color, for even that can be glazed with a still darker tone.

The brilliance of a glaze quite often depends more on the nature of its underpainting than on the strength of its own hue. It should be noted that white, because of its great reflecting power, produces the most brilliant glaze; but, in practice, pure white is rarely used for underpainting. However, white should be a part of practically every color mixture that is to receive a glaze. The only pure, unmixed color I can think of for underpainting is vermilion. For a strong yellow, flake white mixed with hansa yellow or cadmium yellow is best; for blue, prussian blue or ultramarine blue and white should be the choice.

It is apparent, therefore, that the reflecting power of the underpainting and the brilliant appearance of a glaze are interdependent.

Glazing Technique

Glazing onto a wet surface is difficult and requires great skill, since this operation must be carried out swiftly with but one stroke of a brush or knife. Only the softest of brushes or an extra-elastic palette knife should be used, in order to prevent the darker top color from becoming intermixed with the underlying lighter color. Such

a manipulation can be successful only when the paint possesses great viscosity (hence not much mobility) and the capacity to attach itself firmly to the support.

Scumbling

Painting light colors into dark colors in a semitransparent manner is referred to as scumbling. Glazes used in abundance weaken the general appearance of a painting because of their thinness and lack of opacity, but scumbling does not have this effect. It would be just to say that glazing is related to water-color painting, whereas scumbling is intrinsically an oil-painting technique. It relieves dark, opaque areas of gloom or dullness and, if skillfully used, produces liquid effects of light. To illustrate this point, consider painting a light color onto a light surface and the same light color onto a dark surface. In the first instance, the color passage will prove to be rather ineffective, while in the second the sensation of light will be strong and instantaneous.

Scumbling can be done (1) on a dry surface, (2) on a surface that has been covered with a dark and wet glaze, and (3) into a wet layer of paint.

The first is the procedure most generally used, namely, to brush some thin, light color onto a dark paint surface previously moistened with the medium. This is demonstrated in figure 68*A* (top).* The permanence of such a passage may easily be imperiled, however, for such paint applications may prove to be vulnerable to damage in cleaning. Moreover, a very dark underpainting can, in time, "swallow" a frail, light paint on top of it, a phenomenon that can be detected in many of the old masters' paintings. Take, for example, Rembrandt's "Night Watch." Originally, on the top right side of the background many details of the building were visible, if we may judge from a contemporary copy of the painting done in water color, which is preserved in the Rijks Museum, Amsterdam. Today, this part of the painting, after a cleaning which made many previously obscure parts visible again, appears rather dark. In another painting by Rembrandt, "Saul and David," in the Mauritzhuis in The Hague, the composition suffers because the large area of darkness on the upper right side of the painting fails to establish a proper harmony between the figure and the surrounding space. I am quite convinced that some design made in light scumbles must have become lost in this area.

The second kind of scumbling is worked into a wet glaze. A typical instance might be given in which the underpainting is of a dark

* *See page 223.*

168

red color. Upon this ground a glaze of an identical, related, or perhaps a contrasting dark color is applied. Into this wet glaze the scumble is brushed lightly or—an even more effective method—put in with a palette knife. The scumble becomes conditioned by the glaze, and this creates veil-like, soft effects of great beauty. However, the technique of scumbling into a wet glaze does not achieve the greatest permanence.

In figure 68B (bottom) a light color was swept with a few strokes of an elastic palette knife into a solid, dark, and wet layer of paint. Paint of considerable viscosity is needed to execute such passages successfully, and such paint can be produced only with a polymerized, resinous vehicle. Scumbles applied in this manner will possess maximum permanence.

As for the tools used for scumbling, let us consider, for example, how to put a wet scumble into a wet and normally thick paint layer. Any of a variety of soft brushes can be used, as well as the palette knife. However, a brush with stiff bristles would disturb the underlying surface and make the delicate scumbling operation impossible.

Summary: Glazes and Scumbles

It is essential to rub in some of the painting medium before glazing or scumbling.

Any opaque color, when sufficiently diluted with the medium, is suitable for glazing. The transparent colors require less thinning and are also, as a rule, more brilliant.

The color of the underpainting will strongly influence the color of the glaze.

Glazes are, not commonly, painted into a wet paint layer, but if a medium of proper viscosity is chosen this becomes feasible.

Scumbling is more effective if done into a wet glaze or a wet paint surface.

The viscosity of the paint medium and its capacity to affix the paint firmly onto the support are of prime importance.

13

THE NATURE OF PAINTS
AND STABILIZERS

Characteristics of Pigments

GRINDING PIGMENTS in the studio is an indispensable operation for anyone who wants paints with qualities different from the commercially prepared short tube colors. Many writers on the subject of oil painting, as well as the manufacturers themselves, praise the "uniform brushability" of paint as if it were a particular virtue. The fact is that different paints, because of the nature of the pigments involved, vary naturally in texture and consistency. To bring about uniformity in those characteristics is to deprive the paints of their individuality and to level off, as it were, their temperaments. It has been my experience that the more one permits a paint to retain its native quality, the more it lends itself to specific, appropriate uses. That the old masters' paints retained their original characteristics hardly needs to be reaffirmed. Their paints were ground, as a rule, in raw oil, but they were also tempered with resinous and polymerized oils, as described earlier in the book.

Shortness of Paint and Related Deficiencies

Neutral oil, aluminum stearate, wax, an excess of turpentine, and the presence of water and inerts, such as aluminum hydrate, silicate, barium, and so forth, will produce paint of short quality (see figure 69 [top]).*

Too large an addition of inerts also lowers the tinting capacity of paints. Paints that contain too much wax are liable to remain too

* *See page 224.*

170

soft. (Pure wax paint—that is, encaustic—is another matter; since it is not oil paint, we shall not consider its merits here.) Paints which contained an excessive quantity of water were made by some European manufacturers in the nineteenth century with water as a suspension agent; these always fared badly, inasmuch as shrinking of the paint body developed and cracking of the paint became unavoidable. Shrinking of the paint body can also be caused by excessive mixing of turpentine with paints used pastosely.

Conditioning of Paints

Because of the amount of time it requires, many artists cannot prepare their own paints; however, they can easily add Copal Concentrate to the commercial tube colors placed on the palette before starting to paint. In most instances this conditioning rids the paints of their short quality. Sometimes, however, the presence of aluminum stearate proves to be a deterrent in making the paints long; furthermore the intrinsic nature of some paints makes them tend naturally toward a short (or long) consistency. Generally speaking, the precipitated colors—that is, colors containing quantities of inerts, such as aluminum hydrate, barium, clay, and the like, as well as viridian green, chrome oxide green (dull), cadmium yellow, and manganese blue—are by nature short in their quality. Those which tend to become long are: white lead, the mars colors, naples yellow, zinc yellow, and vermilion.

As demonstrated at the bottom of figure 69, certain and sometimes most desirable effects can be produced with long paint alone. Thus fine lines can be drawn in high, smooth-edged impasti, and pastose brush strokes can attain a mellow configuration.

The Stabilizers

1. *Aluminum Stearate.* The presence of this suspension agent in commercial tube paints need not be looked upon as detrimental to their permanence if it does not exceed 2 per cent in quantity. In instances where a paint forms a hard and brittle film, aluminum stearate imparts a certain degree of elasticity to it and, in fact, improves the quality of the paint film. A report on this subject was given by Mr. Henry W. Levison, Director of the Research Laboratories of Permanent Pigments in Cincinnati, at the meeting of the Federation of Paints and Varnish Production Clubs of Chicago, Illinois, in November, 1945. Mr. Levison described tests made over a period of eight years on the proportion of aluminum stearate in paint films prepared with artists' colors. Mr. Levison's project is one

of the few systematic pieces of research on fundamental artists' oil-color formulas. Here are some interesting notes from his paper:

The Effect of Aluminum Stearate on Embrittlement of Highly Pigmented Oil Films:

". . . Tests were made on artists' paint grinds containing varying proportions of aluminum stearate and then compared with grinds of just pigment and oil. Films of the paints were exposed on a flexible support at normal thickness and aged under normal conditions of temperature and indirect light exposure. The changes with time in the hardness, flexibility, and adhesion of the paints were recorded and tabulated.

"The results in regard to durability of the paint films proved interesting in several ways. It was found that not only was aluminum stearate not injurious to durability, but it quite definitely improved the flexibility and adhesion of the more 'oil hungry' pigments like ultramarine and viridian. Aluminum stearate had a very noticeable plasticizing effect on the oil film, preventing it from becoming too hard and brittle, although the drying was not impaired. Aluminum stearate was also found to improve the outdoor durability of the paints.

"Beeswax, a traditional material for this purpose, was also tested. Beeswax did improve flexibility in the first few months, but after eight years the paint film behaved as if the beeswax had never been added. That is, the plasticizing effect of the beeswax had entirely disappeared and the paint was just as brittle as the one without aluminum stearate."

Although I formerly advocated a method of incorporating aluminum stearate with hand-ground paints that was suggested to me by the eminent expert on drying oils, the late Dr. Maximilian Toch, I have found that mulling of the materials into the paint paste was not quite successful, for in many instances the suspension of pigment in oil did not last over a year. It seems that only mechanical methods such as those used by the paint manufacturers can insure a thorough incorporation of aluminum stearate with paints and thus preserve them indefinitely in a usable condition in tubes.

Because of this limitation, I have experimented with many other substances and, after making exhaustive tests, decided to use, instead of aluminum stearate, the pigment known as raw green earth (terre-verte) which has proved to be a most satisfactory suspension agent. For use in studio-prepared tube color, this, in my opinion, gives the maximum assurance that pigments and oil will remain in perfect suspension for years.

2. *Green Earth as a Stabilizer.* Green earth, although its color differs radically from some of the colors with which we mix it, has

only slight tinting power. As much as one-fourth of this pigment (by bulk) can be added to vermilion, for example, without affecting the hue of the latter. Of course, green earth will not alter the hue of the green or blue colors at all, even if added in considerably larger proportions. If the ratio of green earth is increased by more than one-half in bulk, the hue of vermilion goes down, and the resulting paint is of a delicate light red color which might become a valuable addition to the painter's palette. A color mixed in this manner has a tint not unlike some varieties of terra pozzuoli which I have not been able to obtain in many years.

When green earth is mixed with iron oxide red (venetian red), the resultant hue is a very beautiful mild, grayish red, most useful in painting flesh tints.

Naples yellow, which may easily become too runny in grinds, will improve in this respect when mixed with green earth, and its hue will turn greenish. In preparing mars yellow and mars orange, both of which possess the texture of fine dust and require but a brief workout with the palette knife, the admixture of green earth is indispensable; it does not affect the hues of the mars colors at all, and immeasurably improves their suspension in oil. A normal grind of mars orange, for example, which would turn to the consistency of semihardened mud when left on the palette for a few days, retains suppleness and excellent brushability with the addition of green earth, and becomes suitable for storing in tubes.

In the use of green earth as a stabilizer, there can be no possible question as to its compatability with all the other pigments in point of chemical reaction, for it is totally inert and not reactive with any other color. Nevertheless, on general principles it should be ground separately in linseed oil and then intermixed with other colors, for when ground in oil, each of the pigment particles is covered with an oil film which affords it a good insulation. In other words, one should avoid mixing the pigments in dry form to prevent the particles from intimate contact with each other.

3. *Wax as a Stabilizer for Paints.* Wax also can be used as a stabilizer. To incorporate it with oil, a small quantity—let us say a quarter of an ounce—should be dissolved in three to four teaspoonfuls of turpentine and added to ten ounces of hot linseed oil. This represents about a 2 per cent wax-oil relation, considered sufficient for stabilizing paint.

The originally clear mixture appears cloudy upon cooling. Before you incorporate the wax-oil mixture with pigments, it should be heated and poured into a preheated mortar made of unglazed porcelain. This is done to effect an even distribution of wax throughout the oil and also throughout the body of paint. When grinding paints

173

in a mortar, an unglazed pestle should be used for a more effective dispersion of the pigment in oil.

Summary: Nature of Paints and Stabilizers

Neutral oil, aluminum stearate, and wax produce a short paint.

Certain colors are short by nature, while some have the tendency to become long.

All tube paints require conditioning with Copal Concentrate to ameliorate their short quality.

Aluminum stearate is the most generally used stabilizer; it also improves the elasticity of some paints.

In studio practice, raw green earth is preferable to aluminum stearate or wax.

14

GRINDING PAINTS

IF A PAINTER wishes to grind his pigments himself, he needs considerable technical knowledge, for an understanding of the nature of the oils and pigments to be combined is necessary to achieve quality in the resulting paints.

The oil absorption of pigments, though it depends to some extent on the quality of the individual pigment (that is, the method of manufacture and the type of linseed oil used), may be expected to be fairly consistent. Therefore the following table should prove useful. It gives the oil requirements of the principal colors, in the sequence of their quantitative absorption from least to most, measured by weight.

Oil Absorption of Pigments

From 9% to 25%: White lead, vermilion, naples yellow, zinc white.

From 25% to 50%: Cadmium-barium yellow and red, chrome oxide green opaque, c. p. cadmium yellow and cadmium red, cerulean blue, indian red, zinc yellow, venetian red, titanium oxide, mars violet, ultramarine blue, strontium chromate yellow.

From 50% to 80%: Yellow ocher, mars yellow, raw sienna, cobalt blue, raw umber, viridian green, burnt sienna, burnt umber.

From 80% to 100%: Ivory black, prussian blue, raw and burnt green earth.

From 150% to 210%: Alizarin crimson, phthalo green, phthalo blue.

The Body of Pigments

The degree of a pigment's oil absorption is in good measure responsible for the characteristics of its body. Let us take, for example, the extremes—white lead and alizarin crimson (the first requiring 9 per cent oil, the second 150 per cent). When mixed with Copal Concentrate, white lead in a thickness of one-eighth of an inch forms a skin in a few days and solidifies throughout in a few weeks. Alizarin crimson, on the other hand, does not form a skin in a matter of many weeks, and it takes many months to dry throughout. If it is mixed with linseed oil alone, the process of oxidation is considerably prolonged.

The oil absorption of phthalo blue as compared to prussian blue is also characteristic and should show (in part) why the difference in nature of these two colors is so marked. Therefore, in choosing colors for use in underpainting, one should keep in mind that paints of lesser oil absorption will produce a leaner foundation of the sort upon which overpainting may best be carried out.

Grinding Oil

Raw linseed oil, such as is easily obtained in art-supply stores, should be used for the grinding of most pigments. The cold-pressed type of linseed oil, traditionally used, is at the present time unobtainable in this country; instead an alkali-refined oil is offered which, in the opinion of experts, is supposed to equal the former in all respects. At any rate this oil should be neutral and unpolymerized, except in a few instances where a thickened oil appears to be preferable.

Because the amateur color grinder will not wish to be encumbered with chemical paraphernalia, he can very well test his oil by the smell; a sweet smell will indicate that the oil is fresh and a characteristically rancid odor will point to the presence of free acid in the oil. The more air has access to the oil, the quicker free acid will develop. Heat, also, will accelerate acid development. Free acid can be neutralized by adding a tablespoonful of pulverized quicklime to a pint of oil and heating it on an electric plate for about half an hour with frequent stirring. There is no need to pour off the oil, for the calcium oxide which settles at the bottom of the bottle after the processing becomes converted into calcium soap.

176

Polymerized Grinding Oil

The painter may find the manipulation of pigments somewhat difficult in this viscous oil which makes the grind hard to move. The viscosity is in proportion to the degree of polymerization, and hence only lightly polymerized oil should be used, oil which has been exposed to the rays of the sun for only a few days. This exposure to sun should take place in summertime, and it should be done in a shallow pan filled with the oil about half an inch deep. The pan should be covered with a piece of glass to keep the oil clean. If a lead pan is used the oil becomes more siccative, and also the mucilaginous substance it contains separates. At least fifty hours of exposure to the sun is necessary to obtain a high degree of polymerization. It is important not to stir the oil while it thickens, for if the mucilaginous sediment becomes mixed with the clear oil, it cannot be reseparated by ordinary filtration. Therefore the oil should be carefully decanted after exposure so that the heavy sediment is left at the bottom of the lead pan.

Colors Requiring the Use of Thickened Oil

Experience teaches us that certain commercial paints are not satisfactory as to texture and viscosity, and hence also lack brushability. Moreover, the drying properties of some paints are deficient, and their linoxyn is weak. Although the addition of Copal Concentrate will greatly improve such paints, when ground in thickened oil their body will become still firmer.

The following pigments can be ground to best advantage in moderately polymerized oil: white lead, barium yellow, zinc yellow, strontium yellow, the cadmiums, ivory black, and alizarin crimson. Copal Concentrate should be added to these colors too before we start to paint.

To improve the quality of commercial tube paints proceed as suggested in the section headed "Paints Useful in Long Condition," toward the end of this chapter.

Tools for Grinding

The use of a muller and a glass plate will be practical only for grinding larger quantities of paint. The muller should be two and one-half to three inches wide, and the plate must be well roughened by mulling into it a heavy carborundum grain, of mesh No. 40 or thereabouts. The abrasive should be mixed with water before it is used on the plate, where it will produce a pebbled surface.

The plate and the muller eventually lose their tooth. Hence repeated resurfacing of these implements is necessary. It is not essential, therefore, to obtain a so-called sand-blasted glass plate. Any heavy plate glass about twenty inches square can be used.

Cleaning the plate and the muller of the paint residue which clings to it tenaciously is tedious work; to facilitate this, the paint should first be well loosened with kerosene and then washed off with soap and water.

If only a small quantity is to be prepared for daily use, one can easily dispense with all this paraphernalia and simply use a palette knife with a short, stiff blade three to four inches long and at least three-quarters of an inch wide for the grinding. These specifications for the blade are important for efficient dispersion of the pigment in oil. The rubbing down of paint can be carried out on an ordinary palette.

Grinding Procedure

The salient points to remember in grinding paint are as follows. A small quantity of pigment (a teaspoonful, for example) should be placed on the palette and enough oil added to produce a rather dry paste. The mixing should be vigorous but brief, and the semidry paste will need a thorough workout with the knife. After prolonged rubbing, the paste loosens up and becomes glossy and more elastic. It is imperative to start working with a stiff paste in order to obtain a proper quantity-relation of oil and pigment. All that grinding really amounts to is the breaking up of the particle conglomerates of pigment; if it is not properly done, brittleness of the paint film may result.

Larger quantities of pigments—a few teaspoonfuls at one time— should be ground with the muller. In this procedure, it is essential to spread the film of the paste so thinly as to permit close contact of the grinding tool with the surface of the glass plate.

If the paint becomes too thin after continuous mulling, more pigment should be added and the paste again thoroughly ground.

After twenty-four hours, some colors may thin down again and a further addition of pigment may be necessary.

Behavior of Colors in Grinding

As I have observed, there is a marked difference in the manner in which pigments react with oil. It should be interesting to review all our pigments with regard to their behavior in grinding.

White Lead

Three kinds of white lead are necessary, none of which need be studio ground. This pigment is hard to prepare, and the painter will not wish to spend a great deal of time in grinding a color himself when there is a quite satisfactory commercial product available.

First, there is the canned type of white lead which comes in paste rather than liquid form and which we use for priming a canvas or panel. This material, however, is prepared with an acid-refined oil and, because of the nature of its vehicle, it is inclined to yellow. For use in priming, this circumstance cannot be considered a serious handicap. The canned paint is cheaper to buy; and, when thinned with Copal Varnish, even for underpainting it sets so firmly that after an hour or two it can hardly be moved with the brush.

The second type of white lead is the standard quality of tube flake white. When a small quantity of Copal Concentrate (a quarter teaspoonful to about three inches of paint as it comes from the tube) is added to it, it stiffens considerably. This can be attributed to its reaction with the high acid value of the resin. The reaction also causes formation of lead soaps that help to bind the pigment into a cohesive film. The stiff white lead can be used directly or it can be thinned with the medium. In both cases it will be characteristically short. However, a considerable addition of the Copal Concentrate will make it long and stringy.

A third kind of white lead can be prepared by draining off the original vehicle and replacing it with a highly polymerized stand oil. Since not much of this material will be used, it is best to place it in a studio-size tube instead of the standard one-pound receptacle.

As previously mentioned, paint which is to be stored in a tube should not be compounded with a resinous vehicle (such as Copal Concentrate, for example), because the acidity of the resin will cause it to congeal.

For the techniques discussed in this book, these whites will suffice. References to other white colors are on page 195.

Blue Pigments

Prussian blue requires considerable grinding. It is best to use the commercial tube paint as there is in this case no particular merit in a studio-prepared color. The same applies to *manganese blue.*

Cerulean blue. It is advisable to try to obtain genuine cobalt and tin oxide pigment and grind it oneself. At least 15 per cent green earth should be ground with it, for it has a strong tendency to separate from the oil.

179

Ultramarine can be mixed with oil to a loose consistency by means of a palette knife. It is a somewhat brittle color. To promote a better suspension in oil, 10 per cent raw green earth can be mixed with it.

Those who may wish to incorporate ultramarine with wax, for which it has an especial affinity, may refer to page 173.

Green Pigments

Viridian green is a hard, glassy pigment. As it is difficult to compound with oil, we may as well forego the effort and use the commercial product.

Chrome oxide green (dull), on the other hand, can be mixed with a palette knife and it does not require a stabilizer.

Yellow Pigments

Yellow ocher, like most of the other earth colors, can be easily prepared. Because of the coarseness of the clay particles, it is well to use a glass plate and a muller. The same applies to *raw and burnt sienna.* (Some qualities of these pigments, however, have a fine texture.)

Mars yellow and *mars orange* require an effective stabilizer, such as raw green earth. An addition of ocher or raw sienna will also serve this purpose well. About 20 per cent of either of these pig· ments will be needed.

Zinc yellow can be ground in slightly polymerized oil with a muller. *Naples yellow* requires but a brief mixing with a palette knife without a stabilizer. The grinding time varies according to the quality of the pigments, also the oil, which as a rule, should be neutral.

Cadmium barium yellow does not require a stabilizer, but it is well to use a stabilizer with the cadmium sulphides. Both these pigments are easy to grind.

Red Pigments

It appears that the less clay the *iron oxide* colors contain, the more liable they are to harden in tubes after prolonged storage. Hence, to prevent the separation of oil and pigment, ocher or raw green earth can be added to *venetian red* in a proportion of about 15 per cent (by weight). Green earth can also be combined with the darker iron oxides *(indian red* and *mars violet).* These colors require a more energetic workout with a muller.

Cadmium barium red and cadmium selenide behave like the cadmium yellows.

Vermilion is a heavy pigment and requires prolonged mulling. After the paint has reached the proper consistency, about a day later it gets runny and more of the pigment has to be added. I have found that, no matter how carefully I compound vermilion with aluminum stearate, after a few months' storage, because of its great density, separation of oil and pigment begins to take place. I therefore advise anyone who does not wish to condition it with green earth to use a fine clay (kaolin) as a stabilizer. First the clay should be mixed with oil and tested on a glass plate to see whether it is too gritty. A coarse clay cannot easily be reduced to a fine consistency by simple mulling, so one should test several samples carefully before deciding on a suitable material.

Clay should be added to vermilion in the proportion of 15 per cent by volume, which may amount to about 5 per cent by weight. (Further reference to vermilion is made on pages 187 and 188.)

Alizarin crimson. The grinding of this pigment (without stabilizer) should be done with a slightly polymerized and neutral oil. When the tube color is used, it should be deprived of its oil content (as described on page 182) and then mixed with Copal Concentrate when placed on the palette.

Black Pigments

Ivory black. The same rule applies here as with alizarin crimson, except that the grinding oil may have a still higher degree of polymerization. No stabilizer is needed.

Mars black, which we see only on rare occasions as a commercial tube color, is an important material, for it is quite different from ivory black in tone, texture, and drying qualities. It should be compounded with raw oil. Use only half the amount of oil that is needed for the preparation of ivory black. A small amount of polymerized oil can be added to the ground color to increase its viscosity. It does not require a stabilizer. Unlike ivory black, mars black must be thoroughly mulled; it also has a tendency to become stringy in a short time.

General Observations on Paints and Stabilizers

All the proportions which have been given concerning relative amounts of pigments and stabilizers are indicated by volume, unless weight is indicated. They represent approximations, not exact figures.

181

When I refer to a stabilizer, it is to be understood that its use is recommended only if a paint is to be stored in tubes. For use in a matter of days, or even weeks, paint should be prepared with the oil alone.

The directions given here have evolved from studio practice. However, the behavior of some pigments may possibly deviate at times from my description; for pigments may vary somewhat in their reaction, depending on the method of their manufacture. Any variation in the chemistry of the grinding oil can also produce a different reaction. The following pigments separate from oil in anywhere from a week to a month, or perhaps a year. In the order of the speed with which they separate from the vehicle they are: mars orange, mars yellow, cerulean blue, vermilion. These are the typical pigments. The others react in a rather unpredictable fashion, and only a few, as a rule, will remain in good suspension in oil for indefinite periods. These pigments are: White lead, barium yellow, naples yellow, chrome oxide green (dull), viridian green, ocher, sienna, umber, ivory black, alizarin crimson.

Paints Useful in Long Condition

Both short and long paints have specific uses. It is impossible to generalize and say which of the conditions is preferable, for it all depends on the painter's personal technique. Some of the most used paints that tend to become long are: white lead, naples yellow, vermilion, zinc yellow, and a number of the mars colors. Tube paints that are extra short can be made long by removing some of the vehicle from the paint and replacing it with Copal Concentrate before painting. To reduce the amount of oil in which the paint has been ground, place it on an absorbent paper, which will eliminate a quantity of the original vehicle. The thinner the paint is spread on the paper, and the longer it is left on it, the more oil will be drained off.

Preparation of Special Colors

Some paints, as I have said, are not put up in tubes, but can be obtained only in pigment form. Lately, however, more and more of these colors have been made available by the different manufacturers. Certain other colors are rarely to be had as genuine pigments. We might also desire to store premixed combinations in tubes for our own future use.

Genuine colors as a rule are difficult to procure. These are naples yellow, vermilion, and cerulean blue. Substitutes for these paints, which match the original colors in tone value, but otherwise radically differ from them, are to be had in tubes.

Colors that are generally not found in tubes are mars brown light and dark, mars black, dark ocher, burnt ocher.

Combinations of colors that can be useful to the painter are ivory black and umber. A small quantity of umber (up to 10 per cent by volume) added to the black will materially accelerate its drying, while hardly altering its intrinsic color value.

A mixture of ivory black, burnt sienna, and ocher will approximate the color of umber, thus serving as a substitute for this valuable paint which, because of its enormous siccative quality, can sometimes become undesirable.

A color of a rather neutral hue is monastral blue. In mixtures with monastral green it produces a very beautiful and clear-toned green-blue glazing color.

In discussing the properties of green earth as a dispersion agent, I mentioned a few more possibilities of color mixtures in combination with this color. The interested painter can enlarge his field of inquiry into the combination of colors by experimenting with green earth and raw sienna, or green earth and ocher or mars yellow. A variety of beautiful greens can thus be obtained, such as are to be seen in many of the paintings of the old masters. It is also logical to assume, because of the relative rarity of the blue colors at that period, that most of the greens of the old masters were mixtures of yellow colors and black, rather than yellow and blue.

Storing Paints in Tubes

When paint is to be put in tubes, grinding with a muller is more efficient than using a palette knife, for larger quantities of paint can be prepared more speedily in this manner.

Present-day tubes are made of aluminum. It is possible to use empty shaving-cream or toothpaste tubes, after cutting off the bottom and thoroughly cleaning out any of the former contents. Tubes should be filled from the bottom. Small quantities of paint should be placed in the tube with a palette knife. Tapping the uncapped end of the tube on the palm of one's hand will cause the paint to settle in the neck of the tube first. When this is done, the cap should be screwed in place and the tube should be filled, always with the precaution of tapping the top of the tube on the palm of one's hand from time to time so as not to leave any air pockets in the tube. The tube should be filled to an inch of the bottom rim, thus leaving an inch of the pliable metal for folding over and closing securely.

Painters who wish to put their ground colors in tubes will be aided by the following table showing the approximate quantities of pigment and oil to make one tube. A very simple working method is suggested here that should be generally applicable. However, different manufacturing methods may produce some degree of difference.

A standard teaspoon is used as the measuring unit. The pigment should be placed in the spoon, tightly packed and level with the sides of the spoon. The oil should fill the teaspoon to the brim.

With the exception of white lead and zinc white, which are best stored in one-pound tubes, all the colors should be put into standard studio tubes.

Color	*Pigment* (teaspoonfuls)	*Oil* (teaspoonfuls)
Ultramarine	17	7
Cerulean blue	12	4
Prussian blue	14	8
Viridian green	11	8
Chrome oxide green (dull)	15	6
Yellow ocher	18	5
Mars yellow	19	8
Zinc yellow	20	7
Naples yellow	16	6
Barium yellow	20	7
Cadmium barium yellow	21	6
Cadmium orange (sulphide)	15	5
Cadmium barium red	20	6
Vermilion	15	6
Raw umber	15	9
Burnt sienna	12	8
Mars brown	20	8
Venetian red	20	10
Indian red	18	7
Alizarin crimson	16	7
Ivory black	13	7
Mars black	24	7

A large tube of white lead takes 18 ounces of pigment and 2½ fluid ounces of oil.

For zinc white, 10 ounces of pigment requires 3 ounces of oil.

*Summary: Vehicles for Grinding Pigments and Preparation of Col-
ors*

The oil absorption of pigments varies from 9 per cent to 210 per
cent, according to the pigment.

Raw, neutral linseed oil is used for grinding paints, but on some
occasions polymerized oil is indicated. Commercial paints are improved by conditioning with copal resin and polymerized oil.

Grinding should be done with a muller on a carborundum-
roughened glass plate; for small quantities, a palette knife and
palette may be used.

Thorough dispersion of the pigment in oil is essential.

The behavior of pigments in grinding is not uniform.

Some paints (to be stored in tubes) will require stabilizers. Some
are more useful in a long condition.

Some colors can be mixed to create a new composite color.

Ground paint may be packed into tubes with a palette knife.

15

THE VIRTUES OF STRONG
AND WEAK COLORS

IN ADVERTISEMENTS of artists' colors, it is common to stress the colors' great tinting strength. A paint that is not adulterated by fillers is thus claimed to be most desirable. In practice, however, this is not always the case, for weak as well as strong colors have a distinct place and lend themselves to specific uses. In some instances colors of great tinctorial power are indispensable. Such colors, for example, are preferable in glazing, where a weak color would be ineffective. On the other hand, a weak color will generally be found more useful in scumbling.

Characteristics of Cadmiums

In the case of cadmium yellow, a weak tint is worthless; that is why adulterated grades of cadmiums should be avoided. Although the cadmium-barium colors are all excellent, the pure cadmium sulphides are, as a rule, preferable because of their stronger tints. It should be noted in selecting cadmium yellow that quite often the price does not bear much relation to the quality of the color offered, and that the higher-priced product is not necessarily the best.

Cadmium red should be a pure cadmium selenide rather than the cadmium-barium, since it is important to preserve the brilliant hue of this color and generally to safeguard its identity, whereas cadmium yellow enters into many color mixtures where it often loses its identity in creating an entirely new color.

Cadmium orange, in my experience, is more advantageously used in the cadmium sulpho-selenide form.

Other Yellow Colors

Important as it is to possess a yellow color of great tinting strength, at times it is necessary to have at one's disposal a yellow high in key but weak in tinctorial power, for example, strontium yellow.

Zinc yellow is another useful paint, weaker in tint than the cadmiums and considerably less clear in tone. This means that in mixtures it produces "muddy" tones, a condition not necessarily undesirable if its nature is fully understood. Apart from their difference in color value, zinc yellow can easily be changed to an extra-long paint, whereas the cadmium barium and especially the strontium yellow are particularly short.

Naples yellow and barium yellow, although they possess similar color value, represent another contrast in opacity and tinting strength. (When referring to barium yellow, I have used as my standard the paint produced by Permanent Pigments. This pigment differs with different manufacturers.) Naples yellow, which is a pigment of great importance to our palette and which is identical in color and textural aspects to the ancient lead-tin yellow, is equal in opacity to white lead. Since it is a lead pigment, it easily becomes long in the presence of polymerized oil, even exceeding white lead in this respect. Because, as a tube color, it is mostly adulterated, one should employ only a product designated on the label as "lead antimoniate." Barium yellow, on the other hand, is an exceedingly short and fine-textured paint possessing very slight tinting power and no opacity at all. It is most suitable for scumbling. However, to be suitable for use, the tube paint should be well mixed with Copal Concentrate. As with ivory black, I prefer to eliminate much of its original vehicle (by placing the paint on absorbent paper) and then mix it with Copal Concentrate. In contrast to naples yellow, barium yellow is a very poor dryer.

Characteristics of Vermilion

Vermilion is a relatively rare color; only a few manufacturers supply a true sulphide of mercury paint. In most instances, the term "vermilion" designates a color value rather than the genuine pigment. Vermilion is not a color that one uses frequently and habitually, and a tube of it goes a long way. Therefore it is advisable to grind the pigment in the studio.

187

The importance of vermilion as a tinting agent is demonstrated by the fact that it conditions the tonality of other colors in short order when brought into play with them, whereas the best of cadmium reds tends to lose ground and its hue yields in a similar situation.

Other Red Colors

Venetian red, the artificial iron oxide, is too powerful for general use. In painting flesh tints, for example, the milder light red, or terra pozzuoli, pigments, which contain large proportions of clay, are far more agreeable. Indian red and mars violet, the latter known in older nomenclature as *caput mortuum,* are almost pure dark iron oxides. Their aggressive tints make them still more difficult to use, for, like the chrome oxide green (dull), they seem to annihilate any other color on the palette.

The Blue Colors

With the exception of flesh tints where the much milder and weaker ultramarine is no doubt preferable, prussian blue answers most of our requirements. Its very great tinting capacity and its particularly beautiful green hue make it a universally adaptable color. Manganese blue is too weak to serve any other purpose than that of a siccative agent. Cerulean blue, which (when genuine) has a good tinting strength, can be of value only when mixed with a much weaker color so as to safeguard its identity.

The Monastral Group

We may say that monastral blue and green can be considered counterparts of prussian blue and viridian green. In spite of the fact that they are greatly reduced with extenders, the tinting capacity of these colors is extraordinarily strong. Therefore, they lend themselves especially well to glazing and to influencing radically any other color or color combinations. Moreover, as compared with the clear tone of monastral green, viridian appears almost muddy. On the whole, however, the monastral colors are not often used.

Mars Colors

Although they are all very powerful, here a distinction must be made between the light colors, yellow and orange, and the dark varieties, brown, red, and black. Whereas the former, because of their fine-textured body, lend themselves to thin applications, the latter, because of their coarseness and tendency to become long, are exceptionally well suited for use in strong impasti. The dark mars colors are strong and should, as a rule, be used only in mixtures among themselves.

Mars Black

This color, once its nature is understood, can become of great value to the painter. Though distinctly different from ivory black, mars black can be substituted for it where maximum opacity, tinting power, or considerable pastosity are required. In combination with ochers, cadmiums, and white, it can be used for producing very interesting gray-greens.

The "Domineering" Team

In the process of painting, the necessity often arises for a radical altering or neutralization of a color or color combination already placed on the canvas. Radical influencing of any color while painting wet-in-wet can be accomplished in the direction of a warm tonality with an addition of venetian red, and in the direction of a cold tonality with an addition of chrome oxide green (dull). These colors may be considered, next to the mars and the monastral paints, as possessing the greatest tinctorial power.

Characteristics of White Colors

There is no valid reason why we should use zinc white in our painting, unless a slower drying white is needed. White lead has the all-round qualities we desire such as a firm body, excellent drying capacity, and the right tinctorial power in mixtures with all the other colors.

The color strength of the titanium oxide mixtures so popular nowadays is, in my opinion, a doubtful advantage, for their strong reducing capacity can weaken the hue of other colors too radically. However, the great hiding power of titanium white pigment can be useful in the preparation of gesso in combination with whiting in the priming of panels.

Reflective Qualities of Paints

It is also of interest to mention the reflective qualities of various

189

paints as recorded and reported to me by Mr. William Payne. The paint used in the following experiment was applied pastosely, just as it came from the tube, and the reading was recorded with a General Electric Light Meter held at a distance of three inches from the paint samples. Artificial light was used in order to keep the readings at the lower end of the light-meter scale, where finer gradations are marked.

RELATIVE POWERS OF REFLECTION IN ARTIFICIAL LIGHT

Paint	Foot Candles	Paint	Foot Candles
Zinc white	12.5	Burnt umber	3
White lead	12	Chrome oxide green (dull)	3
Cadmium yellow (light)	9.5		
Cadmium yellow (deep)	8	Viridian green	3
Naples yellow	8	Cerulean blue	3
Vermilion	6	Ivory black	2.5
Cadmium red	5	Alizarin crimson	2.5
Yellow ocher	5	Raw umber	2
Venetian red	4	Prussian blue	2
Maganese blue	4	Ultramarine blue	2
Indian red	3	Phthalo blue	2
Burnt and raw sienna	3		

Test for Tinting Strength of Colors

A simple method is generally used to establish the relative strength of colors. Two holes of equal size, about half an inch in diameter, should be drilled in a board that is about a quarter of an inch thick. One should be filled level with one of the colors to be examined, the other hole with white lead. Mix these two together and repeat the process for the other color. The resulting tints of the two colors may be compared for their relative strength. In such a test, an inferior sample of cadmium yellow, for example, will appear pale, as compared with a cadmium of better quality.

Test for Color Fastness

To test a color for its resistance to light, brush it onto a small area of a panel and let it dry. Cover half of this sample with tinfoil and expose the whole to sunlight for six hundred hours. Then compare the two sections of the sample for any change in the appearance of the color. Six hundred sun-hours are accepted as conclusive proof of a color's behavior in regard to lightfastness.

Summary

Both strong and weak colors have definite uses in painting.

For glazing, and for the radical altering of any given color scheme on the canvas, colors possessing relatively greater tinting power are preferable.

Cadmium yellows and reds must have maximum tinting power to be useful and therefore should be carefully purchased.

Vermilion possesses greater tinting capacity than the pure cadmium selenide red.

The powerful venetian red and its counterpart, the weak light red, or terra pozzuoli, should not be considered as interchangeable; they have different uses.

Prussian blue is the most versatile blue color.

Monastral blue and monastral green are transparent and possess great tinting strength.

The dark mars colors should be mixed mainly with one another, as they have not much color affinity with other paints. Mars black is quite different from ivory black in texture, drying, density, and depth of color.

Strong colors, such as venetian red and chrome oxide green (dull), because of their extraordinary hiding and tinting capacity, are useful for neutralizing any given color scheme when painting wet-in-wet.

Of all the white colors, white lead has the all-round qualities which best serve our purpose.

The ability of the various paints to reflect light differs; a table of reflection values is given.

The tinting strength of colors can be examined by comparing samples that were reduced with white.

A color is considered lightfast if it is unchanged by six hundred hours of exposure to the action of the sun's rays.

17

THE DRYING OF PAINTS

Acceleration of Paint Drying

EXCEPT FOR MEETING the deadlines involved in commercial work, a painter would rarely find it necessary to resort to siccatives to promote the drying of his paints, although every artist has experienced impatience while waiting for his paintings to dry so as to be able to go on with overpaints. However, I have found siccatives indispensable in class work, where a painting has had to dry enough for further work from one day to another. (In speaking of dryers, I have only cobalt siccative in mind.) In my own practice, I do not use a siccative other than umber or manganese blue paint. When one is painting thinly with Copal Painting Medium, the paint film dries reasonably fast without the addition of any metallic dryer. In pastose painting siccative must be ruled out because it promotes too quick drying of the top surface and leaves the paint underneath wet for a long period of time.

When paint is mixed with Copal Concentrate, which does not contain turpentine and which in itself is a relatively slow dryer, and thinned with the copal medium, it solidifies in a short time throughout the mass to a rubberlike consistency, which eventually becomes hard, yet retains elasticity.

Drying by Means of Siccative Colors

When painting thinly, especially with slow-drying colors, there are several means of bringing about rapid drying; a small amount of umber should be added to dark colors, little enough so it will not influence their tonality; while light colors should receive a slight addition of manganese blue. Some umber may also be added to the medium which is always rubbed onto the surface prior to painting, in which case we may speak, in effect, of an umber imprimatura. The same can be done with manganese blue, although in this case the imprimatura, because of its faint tint, will be indifferent as a color. Under rather favorable atmospheric conditions, such as low humidity and a temperature of about 70° F., a thin paint film containing minute quantities of either umber or manganese blue dries in less than ten hours.

Drying of Paints Under Various Atmospheric Conditions

In addition to the siccative qualities inherent in some pigments (that is, their capacity to absorb oxygen), there are certain outside factors which greatly influence the drying of paint. These are: (1) the extent of liquid surface exposed, (2) temperature, (3) humidity, and (4) ventilation.

(1) We performed the following experiment to demonstrate that the rate of drying is relative to the thickness of the oil film. We took a standard quality of linseed oil and brushed it thinly onto one glass plate, more thickly on another. The first oil film became dry to the touch in five days, but the thicker film remained wet after two weeks of exposure to identical atmospheric conditions.

(2) The lower the temperature, the slower the drying. Every painter knows by experience that with the changing seasons the capacity of his paints to dry varies. Some paints dry in a matter of hours at a temperature of 90° F., but may take days to dry at 40° F. Exposure to higher temperatures, therefore, seems indicated if one wishes to accelerate drying. However, excessively high temperatures are said to be injurious to a linseed-oil film.

Various early authors mentioned paintings being exposed to sunlight to make them dry rapidly. On the other hand, researchers now tell us that direct exposure to sunlight is deleterious to the permanence of the linoxyn. The apparent contradiction warrants a closer look. As we know, to be considered lightfast a color must pass the test of a six-hundred hour exposure to sunlight. Consequently, for lightfast colors it is heat rather than light which must be considered an injurious agent. Overheating resulting from continued exposure to sun can easily be avoided if the canvas is placed so the sun's rays strike it slantwise. I have often turned a canvas obliquely toward the sun in this manner for intermittent periods, and the paint surface never felt unduly hot to the touch. Under such conditions, the drying of paint is markedly accelerated.

(3) Atmospheric humidity also has a definite influence on the drying of paints. Humidity above 65 per cent retards drying, while humidity under 40 per cent promotes it.

(4) As to ventilation, a circumstance which, as a rule, receives little attention, it too is an important factor in promoting the drying of oils. Try placing a bottle barely moistened with oil at the bottom in a closed cabinet; after a year shut in the cabinet the oil will still feel sticky.

Other Means of Accelerating Drying of Paint

As for making slow-drying paints more siccative without the use of a dryer, it is a good idea to heap them on the palette in small quantities and leave them for a week or two exposed to the action of the air. A skin forms on top of the paint. Remove this, and the paint underneath, because of oxidation and polymerization, will be more viscous and its drying qualities will be improved.

Although quick drying of the underpainting may be pleasant, let me repeat that it is best to refrain from using even the reliable cobalt dryer; instead, one may add some of the siccative colors to the paint and thin it with a little Copal Varnish.

Remember: impasto painting should not be diluted with Copal Varnish, as doing so may deprive a thick linoxyn of the requisite elasticity.

Paint Drying Hazards

As has been stated, the addition of between $\frac{1}{10}$ of 1 per cent and $\frac{1}{5}$ of 1 per cent cobalt dryer to paints is not considered harmful. However, there is no doubt that in practice a much larger proportion of the siccative finds its way into the body of paint. An excess of the dryer makes the paint absorb oxygen rapidly and, as a result, the linoxyn becomes brittle in a relatively short time. A yellowing of colors also develops.

Retarding of Drying

Some painters may prefer to paint from day to day on a wet surface, but this, under normal cicumstances, is hardly possible. However, there are a few precautions the painter may observe to help retard drying. The paint itself has a variable nature. Some paints dry only moderately well when used unmixed, but this characteristic changes when they are intermixed with other slow-drying colors. White lead, for example, acts in a measure as a catalyst in mixtures with other

194

colors. A thin film of white-lead paint dries in about three days. I refer here to the standard tube white lead, for some qualities of commercial paint sold in cans may dry faster because of different manufacturing methods or a different grade of oil used in them. However, when white lead is mixed with ocher, which is also a relatively slow-drying color, the combined colors will set quicker. Therefore, white lead must be banished from the palette of an artist who desires slow-drying paints, and zinc white or zinc-white titanium compounds should be used instead. All the other quick-drying paints will have to be avoided as well.

It should be mentioned that some tube zinc white or titanium white colors have been conditioned by the manufacturer to dry more rapidly. Should this be the case, the pigment will have to be ground in the studio.

Linseed Oil versus Poppy-Seed Oil

It would be difficult to regulate drying by selecting a special kind of oil, for all we have at our disposal is the more or less standard quality of linseed oil and various kinds of stand oil, some of which dry faster, and some more slowly. On the whole, however, there is not much difference in this respect. Cold pressed linseed oil, as I have mentioned, is not at present available in the United States. This, however, is of no great importance; it is said on authority that the now commonly used alkali-refined product is a perfect equivalent.

Although poppy-seed oil is supposed to dry slowly, somehow I have been unable to find a product which behaves as it is supposed to do.

As to stand oil, if a slow-drying quality is required, one should procure a number of different samples and test them for their drying capacity, which may differ, depending on the method used in their manufacture.

Oil of Cloves

Oil of cloves is a chemically complex compound chiefly containing eugenol. Minute quantities of it will retard the drying of paints. Because it has a tendency to soften the underpainting, only one or two drops should be added to one or two inches of paint as it comes from the tube and the same quantity to a teaspoonful of the medium.

Oil of cloves must be used when fresh, for when oxidized it loses its efficiency. Therefore, one should not leave it in half-filled or open bottles. The synthetic product now on the market is not satisfactory and should be avoided.

Slow-Drying Painting Medium

A quick-drying diluent such as Copal Painting Medium should not, of course, be used if one wishes to retard drying, for it will partially counteract the effect of the oil of cloves. However, a more slow-drying, resinous medium can be prepared from the following ingredients:

> a slow-drying stand oil of low viscosity, $\frac{1}{2}$ part
> linseed oil, 2 parts
> turpentine, 1 part
> Copal Concentrate, $\frac{1}{4}$ part.

To incorporate Copal Concentrate with the ingredients, first mix and heat the stand oil and linseed oil, and add the Copal Concentrate to it while hot. When it is cool, dilute the mixture with turpentine and add about ten drops of oil of cloves to one ounce of the compound.

As I have mentioned, in using oil of cloves one should bear in mind that the longer the surface paint remains wet, the more the oil of cloves will act on the lower paint layers, eventually softening them. However, if the oil of cloves is used in minute amounts, no adverse effects will follow.

Humidity and Cold Atmosphere

Humidity and cold air may also be considered as means of retarding drying. In the winter it is not difficult to make use of cold, and humidity can be produced at any time by hanging a wet cloth (a towel, for instance) upon stretchers one or two inches from the wet surface of the painting and parallel to it. An experiment was done to demonstrate this retarding effect of humidity as follows. A coat of white lead was applied to a canvas, and the canvas was left hanging on the wall to dry. At the same time, another canvas, identically treated, was placed in close proximity to a wet cloth. In the first instance the paint dried in three days; in the second, four days.

Drying of Paint and Surface Gloss

The manner in which a painting dries has a definite effect on the surface appearance of the painting. Quick-drying paints remain glossy because their vehicle remains in its original position, as it was applied. In the case of slow-drying paints, the binder usually shifts to the lower layers of the paint strata or else is absorbed through the pores of the underpainting; this causes the paint surface to go dull upon drying.

Summary: Acceleration and Retarding of Paint Drying

Cobalt siccative is the only specific drying agent considered safe, and then only when added to the medium and paint in an amount not exceeding $\frac{1}{5}$ to $\frac{1}{10}$ of 1 per cent. Paint dries faster when: (1) mixed with small quantities of umber or manganese blue; (2) allowed to dry in warm air of low humidity; (3) exposed to oxidation (on the palette) for a few days prior to being used.

To retard drying: (1) avoid quick-drying paint diluents and colors; (2) add up to 2 per cent oil of cloves to paint and medium; (3) expose the painting to cold air and humidity.

Quick-drying paints retain gloss; slow-drying paints, as a rule, dry with a dull surface.

16

NOTES ON SOLVENTS

OCCASIONALLY, if he wishes to clean a painting or to remove some undesirable overpaints, the painter requires certain solvents not commonly found on the studio shelves. Since I have been using some of these solvents only in recent years, they have not been fully dealt with in my previous books. Among these solvents are: acetone, morpholene, alcohol, ammonium hydroxide, saponin, and diacetone alcohol. Mention should also be made here of Xylene, and my own formula for a strong paint remover.

Acetone is an extremely volatile liquid; it boils at 56.1° C. It is one of the important solvents, inasmuch as it acts on the oil films as well as on the natural soft resins, the synthetic resins, and cellulose derivatives. Even shellac is more than 80 per cent dissolved by acetone. A valuable property is its miscibility in all proportions in water as well as in oil. Because of this, and because it makes a good coupling agent for combining the nonmiscible fluids, it is the basic component of all paint removers.

Morpholene is another powerful solvent, one of the few which acts on a thoroughly aged linoxyn. It is miscible with water; its boiling point is 128.9 C.; and it is also a most effective solvent for shellac and waxes.

Alcohol is a product of fermentation. It is also manufactured synthetically under the name of ethanol (ethyl alcohol), or methanol (wood alcohol). The boiling point of these products ranges from 66° C. to 78.3° C. Alcohol is also contained in paint removers since it completely dissolves shellac, certain soft resins such as mastic, sandarac, and elemi, and also many of the synthetic compounds which go into the making of commercial paints. Damar, however, is only partially soluble in alcohol, and copal is totally insoluble in it. The same applies to a thoroughly aged oil film which, contrary to the general belief, does not dissolve under the action of alcohol. Only paint films which contain alcohol-soluble resins or those not of ancient origin are affected by it.

Ammonium hydroxide (or concentrated ammonia water, 28 to 29 per cent concentration) in a weak solution is useful in cutting thin films of oil or grease from paint surfaces. Together with acetone, it forms an extremely powerful solvent. The action of ammonia stops upon its evaporation from the water, since no residue of any kind is left.

Saponin is a glucocide obtained from certain plants such as soapwort, as well as from the bark of the soap tree. It is a white powder which, when stirred into water, forms a foamy solution. It is said to be harmless to the dry paint film. In solution with ammonia it becomes a still stronger agent for certain phases of cleaning.

Diacetone alcohol has lately become one of the favorite media of picture restorers. It evaporates slowly and distills at between 130° and 180° C.; that is, its evaporation is not unlike that of turpentine or mineral spirits. It is miscible with water and most of the organic solvents except the petroleum hydrocarbons. It can be used effectively to regenerate old varnish films, it partially dissolves copal resin and softens the residue to a gel, and it also acts slowly on certain old oil-paint films.

Xylene is obtained from the destructive distillation of coal. It is preferable to all relatively stronger solvents, such as benzene, benzol, and toluene because it boils at 159° C., whereas the boiling range of the other solvents named lies between 80° and 110° C. This is to say that xylene (or xylol, as it is known commercially) remains on the surface of a painting longer, because of its slower evaporation; thus its action on the paint film is more effective. Also, its fumes are less toxic than those of benzene.

Paint Removers

In describing solvents, I have stressed the importance of a low evaporation rate. To retard evaporation by sealing off the liquid surface, stearine (or sometimes wax) is added in commercial paint removers, which makes such solvents unsuitable for use on paintings. In addition, the combination of too powerful solvents makes the action of these paint removers impossible to control. In studio practice, the following formula can be used for the removal of well-dried paint layers.

Acetone, ½ part
Diacetone alcohol, 1 part
Xylol, 1 part
Concentrated ammonium hydroxide, 5 per cent by volume

(For the complete removal of paint and priming from the canvas, *see* page 212).

18

VARNISHES AND VARNISHING

Copal Varnish

COPAL VARNISH is more resistant and hence preferable to damar varnish for certain purposes. As compared with damar, the following characteristics of copal varnish are evident: its film (in the requisite concentration) is thinner and smoother; it dries in a matter of minutes without retaining the slightest tackiness; it does not soften as easily under heat as damar or mastic; and it is more resistant to dirt. Therefore, with the passage of time, its color will appear lighter and fresher than that of damar. It is of great importance that, in a relatively short time, the film of Copal Varnish becomes far more resistant to the action of turpentine or mineral spirits than damar which, as we have seen, always remains soluble, even by such mild agents as these.

Nevertheless, its extra-thin body means that Copal Varnish cannot be looked upon as absolutely permanent. It does not disintegrate easily by itself, as the soft-resin varnishes do, but its removal by gentle rubbing with a solvent is no problem at all. When mixed with paints it does not weaken their film, as damar varnish would, because it incorporates a more durable resin in the paint. Consequently it lends itself to the following uses: (1) thinning of white-lead paint used for priming and of paints used for underpainting; (2) applying imprimaturas; (3) varnishing.

Thinning of Paint

White-lead color should be thinned to the consistency of heavy cream when used for priming, and should be applied in one, two, or even three of the *thinnest* possible layers, the number depending on the roughness of the canvas grain. White lead priming applications may be done on consecutive days; it is not necessary to wait for a thorough drying. When it is to be used on panels, the priming should be diluted with the varnish still more, so as not to retain brush marks when applied to the rigid material.

For thinning the paint in underpainting, which of course always should be done with great moderation, the value of Copal Varnish is immediately apparent. Paint mixed with it sets quickly and adheres to the support with great tenacity; and its solidification is so rapid that it is difficult to smooth out brush strokes one or two hours after the paint has been applied.

Copal Varnish for Imprimatura

Another important advantage of copal solution is that it is the only resin varnish which solidifies sufficiently when used for imprimatura to resist the action of a medium containing turpentine. Thus, when an oil color is thinned with the varnish to the consistency of water color, it feels dry to the touch in less than an hour. In a few days one can rub in Copal Painting Medium (which, as we recall, contains turpentine) before starting to paint, without danger to the underlying imprimatura. A damar-prepared imprimatura not only dissolves easily in similar circumstances; it also yields to the action of turpentine many months, or even many years, after application.

Varnishing Paintings

Copal Varnish is also suitable as a final varnish for paintings. Where little gloss is desired, the varnish can be thinned with 20 per cent mineral spirits or turpentine. Even in this low concentration, it still gives the paint surface good protection. However, Copal Varnish should not be used on a fresh painting. By fresh painting, I mean one which is still "breathing," or absorbing and releasing oxygen forcefully enough to destroy the cohesion of a varnish film resting on top of it. Only when the pores of the oil paint are fairly closed can a varnish application be considered relatively permanent.

When a painting is sufficiently dry, that is, one to three years after it has been finished (depending on the thickness of the paint strata and the nature of the colors), it is well to brush on Copal Varnish, though not before any existing varnish film has been removed. For still greater protection, a few weeks or months later a second varnishing, this time with damar picture varnish, can follow. This procedure, in my opinion, gives a painting the best possible protection, with the exception of the wax-resin discussed on page 203. If the varnishing is carried out according to this plan, under favorable conditions it can last on a painting for two decades. When steam heat, dirt, or excessive moisture causes the soft resin varnish to deteriorate, the picture is still protected by the underlying Copal Varnish.

A mixture of mineral spirits and xylol can be used successfully to remove an old varnish film, provided it is not an oil-resin varnish.

Varnishing Glazes and Fresh Impasti

Although, generally speaking it is of no material consequence how soon a freshly executed painting receives a coat of varnish, glazes not sufficiently hardened may suffer if they are varnished prematurely, inasmuch as they then become incorporated in the varnish film instead of the paint film proper. This, of course, causes the decay of the glaze. When using Copal Painting Medium, however, the danger that the damar varnish used for retouching would soften a fresh glaze is greatly reduced. Moreover, glazes are as a rule shiny and do not require early varnishing. Therefore, in varnishing a fresh painting one need not necessarily cover the entire surface; it will be sufficient if only the dull passages are varnished.

A fresh, strong impasto produced with paint containing an excess of the medium (or Copal Concentrate) should not be varnished until it is solid throughout, which may mean waiting a few weeks. If one does not wait long enough, the relatively solid, but still soft film on top, which rests on a layer of liquid paint, wrinkles as soon as the varnish sets.

Copal Painting Medium as Varnish

The varnishing of glazes and scumbles after they are thoroughly dry can also be done with Copal Painting Medium simply by rubbing some of the medium, thinned in a proportion of one to one with mineral spirits or turpentine, onto such passages with the hand. This procedure will afford good protection to fragile paint films.

Paint strata which show considerable loss of oil through absorption by the lower layers (such areas remain dull in spite of varnishing) should be varnished with Copal Painting Medium, thinned with turpentine (or mineral spirits) in the proportion of two to one or one to one, depending on the case. This kind of varnishing with a medium is commonly referred to as "oiling out." A minimum of the medium is used by taking a little of it out on the finger and rubbing it vigorously into the paint stratum, thus producing the thinnest possible distribution. There is no danger that paint passages treated in this manner will show yellowing. However, on general principles, white surfaces which stay mat in spite of the varnishing should, because of their great sensitivity, be treated with Copal Painting Medium thinned with turpentine or mineral spirits in the proportion of one to five.

Varnishing to Prevent Trickling

As we know, brushing turpentine on the paint film does away with the bothersome condition of trickling. However, a painter familiar with his materials who understands the nature of his painting medium prefers, on some occasions, to use Copal Varnish rather than turpentine. When the medium is rubbed into the surface after the drying of the varnish, its viscosity increases greatly, and this in turn permits an especially effective manipulation of glazes and scumbles. Moreover, it improves the adhesion of the superimposed paint layer and considerably strengthens the surface gloss.

Wax Used for Protection of Paint Surfaces

Varnishing with damar picture varnish and retouching varnish has been described in some of my earlier books. As I have stated many times, the best varnish offers only fair protection, and under the atmospheric conditions that prevail in any industrial city, periodic revarnishing is certain to be necessary. In an endeavor to prolong the life of the relatively fragile resin, we may very well resort to the use of a wax which has excellent properties as a protective surface coating. On fresh paintings, only beeswax should be used; but for paintings more than ten years old which were executed with a medium free of damar or mastic, carnauba wax would seem to be preferable. A soft beeswax finish can easily be removed if it has to come off for any reason (such as to make later corrections. for example); whereas to remove hard carnauba wax requires prolonged rubbing with a solvent such as turpentine or mineral spirits, and such treatment could injure relatively fresh glazes and thin paint applications.

Preparation of Beeswax

It is best to use refined beeswax; if this is not obtainable, raw beeswax may be purified and bleached by being placed in water and heated to just below boiling point. When the wax floats on the surface, it should be lifted out of the water and the impurities which have collected on the bottom of the piece of wax should be scraped off. Repeated several times, this treatment produces a much lighter material. Another method of bleaching wax is to add one-half part of turpentine to one part of wax and heat in a double boiler. Repeated melting and cooling will produce the desired results.

Mineral spirits make a better solvent for wax than turpentine, since the dissolving power of the former on paint films is weaker than that of turpentine. Although small lumps of wax dissolve in mineral spirits without heat, larger amounts may be melted in the solvent, using a double boiler, to produce an instantaneous solution.

To make a paste of the proper consistency, one ounce of beeswax should be dissolved in about two and a half ounces of mineral spirits (of course, measured respectively by weight for the solid and volume for the liquid). If its container is kept well closed, the paste will remain in a usable condition for an indefinite time.

To prepare a resin-wax compound, use as a solvent one part Copal Varnish to one and a half parts of mineral spirits.

Preparation of Carnauba Wax–Resin Compound

Carnauba wax is obtained from leaves of certain Brazilian palm trees; it is harder and has a higher melting point than any other natural wax. Only the best quality, which comes from young, unopened leaves, should be used; it is lighter in color than unbleached beeswax and produces a very light paste.

The first step in preparing the paste is to reduce the wax to small splinters and dust by whittling them down with a knife. The material should then be placed in a tin container and melted over an electric plate. (To avoid combustion, it is best not to work over an open flame.) When the wax liquefies, a few teaspoonfuls of mineral spirits should be added, and the melt should be well stirred. (A larger amount of the cold solvent would make it congeal.) The compound should now be taken off the hot plate and, very slowly, more mineral spirits should be added. In all, it takes one part of wax to three parts of mineral spirits; then three parts of Copal Varnish should be mixed with it. Thus the finished paste will contain more than twice as much of the solvent as the beeswax preparation.

Beeswax Finish on Paint Surfaces

Wax paste may be used on paintings if the varnish is well hardened. A fresh varnish, especially one prepared from a soft resin, yields easily to the action of the mineral spirits contained in the wax paste. Even on a well-dried, varnished surface, the wax paste which has been thinly spread with a cheesecloth should not be rubbed immediately, but left unpolished for a few hours, for a too precipitate, forceful rubbing would remove even a well-solidified resin film. After the waiting period, when the solvent has been largely volatilized, the waxed surface may be polished with a cheesecloth or any soft, lint-free material.

Wax-Resin Finish on Paint Surfaces

In preference to wax paste, I recommend a beeswax-resin paste because it is more dustproof. Paintings which are to receive a wax-resin finish should be at least a year old. If a paint film is made up of glazed areas, an even longer wait is advisable. Because of the tendency of wax-resin to solidify, it is necessary to polish it within an hour of application, for it hardens fast. When using the carnauba wax-resin paste, *polishing must be carried out immediately upon application,* for it sets very rapidly and hardens to a much tougher film than the beeswax-resin compound. Whichever wax is used, only small areas, about six inches square, should be treated at a time.

Observations on the Waxing Process

The advantage of a wax-resin finish is obvious. Not only does it afford the best protection we can devise at present to a paint surface but, like the varnish, it enhances the depth of the colors and imparts an agreeable gloss to the paint film. Dust that collects on its surface can be wiped off, the effect of atmospheric moisture is minimized, and the gloss can be worked up and maintained by repeated polishing.

The only bad feature of a waxed surface is that overpainting cannot be done on it. The wax film must be removed before paint will again adhere to the surface of the painting. Mineral spirits or turpentine will effectively remove the wax; however, as I said before, this operation should not be attempted on a fresh painting.

A carnauba-wax preparation, because of carnauba's inherent hardness, is better than beeswax to use on panels where vigorous polishing is possible. However, hard pressure with a polishing cloth on canvas should be avoided. When polishing around the picture edges, it is well to insert a cardboard under the stretchers; for protection of the canvas beyond the stretcher limits, one should support it with a book or a drawing board over which enough layers of soft paper have been laid to equal the thickness of the stretcher bar. Thus supported, the canvas will not be likely to be damaged from pressure while polishing.

Waxing to Produce Semimat Surfaces

As mentioned before, the only varnish capable of giving protection to the paint surface and not producing a high gloss at the same time, is Copal Varnish thinned with mineral spirits or turpentine in the proportion of one part of varnish to one-fifth part of the solvent. Mat varnishes (containing wax) have proven ineffective. Ozokerite wax, however is a material that can be used on the surfaces of paintings where a mat effect appears desirable, for example, on murals.

Ozokerite is a natural earth wax; it is dazzling white in color, entirely inert, and harder than paraffin. It dissolves in mineral spirits without heating. A 5 per cent solution (the wax measured by weight, the spirits by volume) sprayed over the paint surface will dry to a satiny surface in a few hours. When, in time, the wax coating becomes soiled, it can be removed with mineral spirits and a new one applied.

Synthetic Resins

I am well aware that, in present museum practice in the United States, vinyl acetates and methacrylate resins are widely used for varnishing paintings. These synthetic resin varnishes are said to be nonyellowing and easy to remove when the need for revarnishing arises, which makes them appear desirable for use on museum paintings. I have tested a number of them but remain unconverted; they handle well under the brush, but I dislike their texture, which seems to me somehow not quite sympathetic to the paint surface.

Moreover, whatever the considerations of museum conservators may be in using these varnishes, their presence in the painter's workshop is inappropriate. Until their behavior with oils has been sufficiently explored, they should not become part of the paint body. According to what we now know, a synthetic varnish should be used, if at all, only on completely finished paintings. But who can tell precisely when a painting is "finished" as long as it stands around in the painter's studio? How often does it happen that the painter puts his varnished painting aside, considering it all finished, only to feel, later on, that extensive revisions are needed? As we know, before painting some of the medium is always rubbed onto the canvas; but if we do this and a synthetic varnish happens to have been used on our painting, it would incorporate itself in the paint film, a circumstance at all costs to be avoided. For these same reasons, any synthetic painting medium should be ruled out.

Common Misconceptions Regarding Varnishes

It has been stated in many art manuals that cracks may develop in paintings if they are subjected to premature varnishing. Although I have always denied such a possibility, at one time it appeared to me as not unlikely that a heavy resin-oil varnish, under certain circumstances, could cause such damage. Indeed, it seems theoretically logical that it might do so. However, in practice I have never been able to make a paint film crack, no matter how early I covered it with varnish. I have used freshly dried films of relatively soft paint, such as the natural earth colors, in tests in which I coated them thickly with many layers of damar varnish, Copal Varnish, and a 50 per cent copal-oil solution—and no cracks developed. However, if a strong varnish should be applied to an old and deteriorated paint film, it is quite conceivable that the varnish might pull off the brittle underlying paint which had lost cohesion.

The complaint is sometimes heard that a certain varnish, even though of a reliable make, remains tacky for a long time after its application. Now varnish cannot alter a tackiness of the paint surface that is already present, and one should be quite certain this was not the case before blaming the varnish. However, if a turpentine-prepared varnish is kept in half-filled or open bottles for a long time, it becomes oxidized, thus resulting in poor drying and stickiness. This is another possible explanation of the above complaint.

The sometimes professed objection against painting on a varnished surface is also unjustified. A varnish film between two paint strata is an effective cement which promotes the better adhesion of the paint layers. Moreover, the varnish film will incorporate itself into superimposed paint which is thinned with a turpentine-containing medium.

Summary: Varnishing

Copal Varnish is, in some instances, preferable to damar varnish; it can be used for thinning paints in underpainting, for imprimatura, for varnishing of paintings, and also to prevent trickling.

Copal Painting Medium thinned with mineral spirits can be used for varnishing glazes and dull paint areas.

Wax affords excellent protection to the paint surface. The refining and bleaching of wax can be done by simple means; the formula for wax paste is one part wax to about two and a half parts mineral spirits, the solid wax measured by weight, the liquid spirits by volume.

To produce a beeswax-resin compound, use one part Copal Varnish to one and a half parts mineral spirits.

Carnauba wax–resin compound is prepared by dissolving one part of wax in three parts of mineral spirits and three parts of Copal Varnish.

Paintings may be coated with wax paste alone, but the wax-resin compound is preferable.

Semimat surfaces can be produced by the use of ozokerite wax.

Synthetic resins should be rigidly excluded from the painter's studio.

Premature varnishing does not cause cracks.

19

MISCELLANEOUS OBSERVATIONS

ALTHOUGH I have stated on numerous occasions that water should not be used on paintings, I shall here qualify that advice, for there are some exceptions to the rule. All kinds of paintings may need to be cleaned, those done yesterday, those made ten to fifty years ago, and perhaps even an antique painting. One should consider the age of the painting, the character and condition of the paint surface, and the type and condition of the fabric which serves as a support for the painting. A thorough examination will indicate whether the use of water for cleaning purposes will be harmful or not.

Water in Cleaning Pictures

A cloth, or a wad of absorbent cotton just moistened with water (but by no means dripping wet) and saponin (not soap, which should be avoided no matter how mild it may be) can be used safely on:

1. A relatively fresh painting (and a painting is still fresh after ten years).

2. On a painting which, although of older date, possesses a cohesive, strong linoxyn and has no crevices or openings even as big as a pinhole. (This can be ascertained by holding the canvas against a strong light.)

In the first case, a fresh painting is elastic enough to follow the expansion and contraction of the fabric, if the fabric should become moist. In the second instance, an old or relatively old paint film can be immune to the movements of a fabric if the film is relatively strong and can resist such movements, and the fabric relatively too weak to cause the paint film to crack. It is obvious that a brittle, thin paint film would be literally shattered into a net of crackle if subjected to the motion of a stronger support.

Fabrics, strong or weak, may react in many ways to moisture. Some of them are quite hygroscopic, some less so, depending on the nature of the thread and the type of the weave.

A certain type of surface grime caused by an accumulation of tobacco smoke or the residue of cooking fumes does not yield easily to the action of a mild hydrocarbon solvent. But if such a residue (which inevitably collects on paintings hung in an average apartment dwelling in large cities) is to be cleaned from a relatively fresh canvas, a moist cloth and saponin-water will do good service.

The following experiment demonstrates the efficiency of this cleaning agent. A painting that had hung for ten years in a room usually well filled with tobacco smoke and adjoining a kitchenette developed a deep brown film which covered the entire surface and proved to be resistant to the action of mineral spirits. Xylol, after prolonged application, removed the film from part of the painting. However, because of the excessive rubbing that had to be done in order to dissolve the scum, the solvent attacked the paint film itself. Diacetone alcohol then was tried and removed the grime quickly, but its action was far too strong for the relatively fresh painting. After the first two attempts proved to be too harsh, a wad of cotton moistened with saponin-water freed the paint film of the obscuring dirt without any effort or bad effects in a matter of minutes without any special effort on the part of the person doing the cleaning. Vigorous and prolonged rubbing with any agent, even saponin, should be avoided, for none can be considered mild. The effectiveness of saponin can be increased by adding a little ammonia to the water. *However, one must be certain that the painting to be cleaned was not done on a gesso or a half-oil ground, for such grounds are extremely susceptible to developing a net of crackle when exposed to the direct influence of moisture.*

Before applying a strong solvent to a paint surface, tests should always be made on a small spot at the edge of the painting to determine the degree of the solvent's action.

Factors Concerning the Permanence of Paintings

1. *Canvas.* The excellent state of preservation of certain paintings over a period of centuries and the absence of even the finest crackle must in many cases, be attributed to a particular quality in the weave of the fabric and the manner in which the priming was anchored to them. Rougher fabrics always insure a better attachment of priming than mangled textiles, on which the priming lies like a

sheet and thus is exposed to far greater surface stress. Hence densely woven materials with a coarser nap are preferable to extra-fine and smooth fabrics. This is a factor especially to be considered in connection with impasto painting, for a thin painting, or one executed alla prima, may behave well even on a relatively smooth (though not toothless) support.

2. *Priming.* Present-day commercial primings are rarely prepared with the traditional white-lead oil paint, chiefly because such grounds need a longer drying time while exposed to strong daylight to prevent their yellowing. However, even if this precaution is taken. Some yellowing of a rolled-in canvas is unavoidable. To forestall this, the manufacturers use a priming prepared from titanated pigments grayed with black in connection with synthetic resins and a volatile solvent. Protected as such grounds are by the subsequent layer of paint, there seems to be not much danger of their deteriorating. However, we have no practical experience in this matter, and only time will tell how these commercial grounds will behave in the future.

3. *Paint.* Factors having to do with the permanence of paint were discussed early in the book. However, it is not only the sleek, tough surface of a linoxyn made up of stand oil and hard resin that possesses maximum resistance; the thickness of the paint itself sometimes contributes to its durability. In the course of years numerous surface cleanings will be carried out, and not always by an experienced hand. Hence, a "skinning" of a painting will eventually be likely to occur. Perhaps one of the reasons that some paintings were preserved for posterity in excellent condition is that their importance was not recognized and nobody bothered to keep them clean and polished year after year throughout the centuries.

Storage and Preservation of Paintings

As previously noted, certain atmospheric conditions such as excessive humidity and dry heat are detrimental to a painting's permanence. A moderate humidity of about 50 to 60 per cent and a temperature of about 60° to 70° F. is ideal. One should avoid hanging paintings near radiators or storing them in moist cellars. In the first instance, a desiccation of the paint surface will result; and in the second, excessive moisture will in time develop mildew on the canvas and sometimes also on the paint surface.

Mold

As we know, the glue that serves for preparation of the size is, under normal conditions, hard and brittle and quite resistant to the attack of bacteria. However, when subjected to humidity of above 70 per cent even for a short period, the best of glues will soften and become soggy. Such material then becomes especially susceptible to the attack of mold. Some protection can be given in advance to the size by spraying the back of the canvas with a 5 per cent solution of alum or formaldehyde before beginning to paint.

Once mold has set in, it can sometimes be removed by exposing the affected parts to the action of ultraviolet rays or to the sun. Rubbing these parts with a wad of cotton moistened with a 10 per cent solution of sodium fluosilicate is another remedy. Subsequent elimination of the residue should be accomplished with a cloth moistened with distilled water. Another effective method, especially suitable for use on pastels and water colors, calls for fumigating the picture in an airtight box containing loose crystals of thymol or paradichlorobenzene.

To prevent the growth of mold, the rabet of the frame and the part of the glass which rests on it should be sealed with strips of cloth dampened in an alcohol solution of one of the above-mentioned ingredients.

Protection from Dirt

Of all the hazards to a painting's permanence, dirt seems to be, next to moisture, the greatest. Varnish gives good protection, and a glass would be still better, but glass must be ruled out in framing oil paintings because it influences the textural appearance of paint surfaces unpleasantly and, as a rule, causes a glare which makes parts of the painting invisible. If a painting is not hung on the wall, it is best to wrap it in cloth or paper and protect it from dirt. The fact that a painting that is kept away from light may yellow is immaterial, for this can easily be remedied by exposing it to strong daylight, which bleaches yellowed paint in a matter of days or weeks, depending on the strength of the light. Short exposure of a painting, placed in a slanting position to sunlight (to avoid overheating), will greatly accelerate the bleaching process.

Reclaiming Old Canvases

If a complete removal of the paint and priming is to be carried out, submerging the canvas in boiling water will have immediate effect, provided that the oil-paint priming has not gone through the interstices of the weave; water, by dissolving the glue size, at once separates the priming and the painting on top of it from the canvas.

20

FACTS AND FICTION

Umber

IT HAS BEEN asserted by some authors that umber, when used in underpainting, strikes through and darkens the appearance of a painting. Pure umber, when used in a solid film, not as an imprimatura, has, of course, no place in underpainting and would hardly serve any reasonable purpose, nor would any other dark color equally rich in oil content be desirable for this. Mixed with white, however, umber is an excellent color for underpainting.

Prussian Blue

This color also has a bad reputation in some quarters, and this for reasons which are purely imaginary. I have exposed fresh, hardly dry samples of pure prussian blue, as well as prussian blue in mixtures with white lead, ocher, and other yellow colors to sunlight for a period of six months. The fresh mixture with white lead was the only one to show a hardly perceptible darkening of tone, and I found this agreeable rather than disturbing. A well-dried mixture, however, remained unchanged after more than six hundred hours' exposure to sunlight. Hence prussian blue is, because of its wide adaptability and other excellent qualities such as strong tinting capacity and good drying properties, perhaps the most valuable blue color on the palette.

I have a great fondness for naples yellow and have never experienced its turning green even when handled with a steel palette knife. Nor have I found that its color suffers when mixed with white lead and cadmium yellow, as is sometimes baselessly alleged.

I had always assumed that naples yellow was used by the old masters, especially since I had observed in medieval, Renaissance, and Baroque paintings a yellow which in all respects, and notably in its characteristic conformation, equals naples yellow. A statement made by Raehlmann that he found this pigment in old masters' paintings to be naples yellow by identifying lead in the compound seemed to support my belief, though it was disputed by de Wild. Only recently, the German chemist, Richard Jacobi, made a definite discovery, identifying the pigment by means of spectral analysis as a lead oxide and tin oxide compound. A control examination by Rollwagen and Riedl (University of Munich) confirmed Jacobi's findings. In this country, Gettens has also used spectral analysis to identify the pigment in a fifteenth-century painting, as reported in the *Bulletin of the Fogg Museum of Art,* Volume X, No. 6, pages 190-191. Moreover, by combining tin oxide and red lead oxide in a crucible at high temperature, Gettens synthesized a pigment which visually is indistinguishable from naples yellow. Depending on the quantitative relation of the ingredients, as well as on the temperature, darker or paler shades of yellow, all very characteristic, can be produced. Having been fortunate enough to receive samples of the lead-tin yellow pigment from Mr. Gettens, I compounded it with linseed oil and stand oil and obtained a paint which to all intents and purposes must be considered identical with that found on paintings from the fourteenth to about the beginning of the eighteenth centuries.

It is difficult indeed to explain why this excellent pigment should have disappeared from the painter's palette at that time, nor do we know when naples yellow superseded it, its history as well being obscure. At any rate, meager as the historical references to the lead-tin yellow are, mention of its formulation and preparation by calcining (in connection with the manufacture of colored glass) was made in the Bolognese manuscript which dates from the fifteenth century.

My interest in this matter is understandable, for it has been my desire ever since I first observed this yellow in the old masters' paintings to possess an identical material. It is to be hoped that this compound, which is simple to manufacture, will before long be on the market.

Rubens' Medium

Lately the recipe of a painting medium used by Rubens and mentioned in the writings of Mayerne has found some popularity. The medium (according to Mayerne) consists of venice turpentine, sun thickened linseed oil, and a soft resin varnish. Neither the proportions of the ingredients nor the manner of their preparation is given in the Mayerne account. In today's practice, the balsam, resin varnish, and oil are simply mixed together in the proportion of one-third each. This produces a medium which, although it has excellent properties for fusing paint, lacks toughness. Hence, it cannot be the same medium which Rubens used.

The following is my suggestion for the reconstruction of the compound. One part of sun-thickened linseed oil should be heated to about 450°F., with 10 per cent of a pulverized run copal (the first by volume, the second by weight). In a test to be made after ten and fifteen minutes to see whether the mixture has become homogeneous, a little oil should be taken out and spread on a glass plate. If it turns turbid upon cooling, the heating should continue. The oil in which the resin has been well incorporated should remain clear after the thermal processing, which may last about twenty minutes. While the mixture is still hot, 5 per cent of venice turpentine should be stirred into it and the compound permitted to cool off. Then it can be thinned with up to 50 per cent (by volume) of turpentine.

Wax-Litharge Medium

In a recent publication, a statement was made to the effect that the formula used by numerous old masters, including Rembrandt, Rubens, et al, called for large quantities of wax mixed into a litharge-saturated oil combined with mastic varnish. It is true that such a compound works very well under the brush. However, mastic-litharge mixtures, known as megilp and recommended in some nineteenth-century recipes, were long ago discarded because they unfailingly brought ruin to every painting in which they were employed.

As to wax in the quantities suggested, its presence was never even suspected by any of the experienced restorers who worked on the principal paintings of the old masters. It is common knowledge that when wax is present in an appreciable quantity in a paint film, it easily softens under the action of heat. The use of a hot iron during the process of relining (practically all the old masters' paintings have undergone one or repeated relinings) would instantly reveal such a

215

condition. Moreover, the action of an organic cleaning agent would also point to the presence of a substantial amount of wax in a paint surface.

21

PAINTING TOOLS

EVEN THOUGH this book has been planned chiefly for those who have mastered the elementary problems of paint manipulation and who wish to delve into the intricacies of a more complex paint technique, a somewhat detailed discussion of the nature of the painting tools seems to be in order.

I hold that such knowledge is more reliable than dependence on inspiration, for, whereas inspiration cannot be controlled, the tools by which it might be released are controllable. In fact, the right tool properly used may be responsible for the ultimate realization of an inspiration. One should keep in mind that the painter's tools— that is, his brushes and palette knives—influence the nature and character of the paintings' texture, and in a large measure are as personal as the painter's signature.

The Bristle Brush

In some of my former writings I praised the superiority of a brush made of "toed-in," or interlocked, bristles—in other words, of bristles which curve from the outside toward the middle of the brush (see the first brush in figure 70).* I also stated that such a brush is of superior make and preferable to the cheaply produced, ordinary brush. With some change in technique in relation to paint textures, however, my former viewpoint has undergone modification in this

* *See page 225.*

216

matter. I have found the "inferior" brush at times eminently acceptable especially in a technique which depends more on "frayed" brush stroke rather than on a precise one (see second brush in figure 70).

Anyone who has used cheaper-grade brushes knows that the "stray" bristles which stand apart at the sides of the ferrule (that is, which do not have a chisel-like shape) produce soft, rather fuzzy contours without much blending. In certain techniques this is a marked advantage. Of course, even the most rigid contour can be blended with a few strokes of a sable brush, but the transitions thus produced are gradual and have a more mellow appearance. The transitions produced by the fuzzy brush, however, have an entirely different character, for the single bristles sticking away from the body of the brush drag some paint along, thus creating a web of interlaced colors. The "turbulent" effects produced by such an imperfect brush create an impressionistic rather than a classic quality of paint surface.

The same applies to the round sable brush (see figure 70 [right]). Here the brush with the perfect point appears to be just as desirable as the one that cannot be brought into any semblance of tapering off. Painters brought up with respect for the pinpoint brush feel that once this advantage is lost the brush becomes worthless. This is not so. Only brushes with too short hair (either from wear or faulty manufacture) or hair that becomes too brittle and breaks off or loses its hold in the ferrule become useless.

The Sable Brush

A sable brush may be a special favorite with the painter inasmuch as it can produce effects that cannot be duplicated by any other instrument.

I am inclined now to assign more importance to the round sable brush and the knife in producing final effects on the canvas than I did at one time, for these tools are capable of relaying faithfully the impulses of the painter's hand with utmost directness and the least impediment.

The round sable brush (figure 70 [right]) is like a writing tool because of the ease and fluency with which it can be made to move over the paint surface. This type of brush is the kind to use on a surface that affords minimum resistance, that is, on a canvas well covered with paint or priming. Any appreciable protuberances of the grain of the fabric inevitably reduce the fluency of the brush strokes and hence impair their capacity to articulate.

In considering the round sable brush, there can be no quarrel with the larger sizes. It is the small brush (Nos. 1 to 10) which is, as a rule, at fault. To a van Eyck, for example, the standard small brush commonly used today would appear ludicrous (see figure 71, the third from the left). For drawing with a diluted paint it is adequate, but it cannot be properly used with a long paint, for any pressure exerted with it would in one operation wipe the paint off, instead of depositing it on the canvas. Fine, pastose hairlines can be made only if the hair of the small, round brush is at least from half an inch to one inch long. Painting with such a brush is like entwining a thread, the thread being the stringy paint which has a more resiliant body than the brush.

Other Useful Brushes

No matter how much one technique may differ from another, in some points it is bound to rely on the same manipulations. Thus, a soft flat sable brush or a blender may be used only in very limited areas by some painters, but be extensively used by others. No matter how different the techniques of painters, they will all need practically every type of brush, with the exception of the small, flat sable brushes a quarter of an inch or less in width. Such brushes are suitable only for paintings of a miniature character. The small bristle brush, up to about No. 4, can be used chiefly for making harsh demarcations, that is, drawing with paint, rather than for painting.

Flat sable brushes are used in the main for the blending of colors where, because of the low viscosity of the paint, a delicate operation is required. When the paint on the canvas has attained a high degree of viscosity, blending can be done very well with a bristle brush. This requisite comes about when painting with Copal Painting Medium; for, after a certain length of time, the turpentine evaporates from the body of the paint and the resin starts to "set."

Flat sable brushes need not be larger than three-quarters of an inch. Brushes of a greater width can be made of soft hair (squirrel and the like); they are useful merely for delicate blending of colors (see figure 71 [extreme right]). The soft-hair blender, as it is called, can manipulate only the top surface of a wet paint layer when the brush is moved rapidly in fanlike motion over the paint surface. Its hair is too flexible; therefore it has not the capacity of agitating viscous paint.

Palette Knives

Every one in the large array of knives (figures 72, 73, and 74) serves a definite purpose and is useful for one or several operations.

Knife No. 1 (figure 72) serves for grinding certain pigments with oil. The blade of this knife is 3 inches long, and ¾ inch wide, and rather stiff, so as to allow maximum pressure for breaking up the particle conglomerates of pigments. The 4-inch knife, No. 3 (figure 72), is also suitable for use in grinding. These knives are called spatulas; they are generally obtainable in stores specializing in laboratory equipment. Such a sturdy knife can also be used for scraping paint from the palette.

Knife No. 2 (figure 72) was made from a spatula 1 inch wide. The long edge of the blade, cut on the bias, is especially adapted for sizing the canvas with glue-gel and for priming with white lead. The blade is 6 inches long; its width at the broadest point is 1 inch, and at its tip ¼ inch. For speedy priming and sizing of large surfaces, the length of the blade can be up to 10 inches. All priming knives should have only moderate elasticity.

Knives 4 and 5 in figure 72 and 6 and 7 in figure 73 are used in underpainting. No. 4 serves for small-size canvases and the proportions of the blade are as follows: length, 3¼ inches; width at its broadest point, ½ inch; at its tip, ¼ inch. No. 5: length, 3 inches, width at the tip, ⅛ inch.

Knife No. 6 (figure 73) is an instrument terminating in a point thin enough to permit precise operations in a very small area. The blade is 3½ inches long and ⅛ of an inch wide at the tip.

Knife No. 7 (figure 73) serves for smoothing larger areas of paint; this is done by holding the blade parallel to the paint surface, not edgewise. The length of the blade is 5 inches, and it is only moderately flexible; but, because the thickness of the blade is almost the same all over, it bends away more easily than the other knives which are made of a steel thicker at the handle and thinner at the end. Whereas, for example, No. 4 makes contact with the canvas on a surface of about 1 inch (the rest of the blade being almost inflexible), No. 7 is in contact with the canvas for 3 inches.

Knives used in underpainting should not be too flexible to force the paint into the grain of the canvas. However, a knife which is too rigid is useless.

In connection with the underpainting, it should be noted that small details (such as painting of the features in a portrait, for example) should be done with a brush first. The knife can then be used for pressing the paint into the grain of the canvas.

Knives Nos. 8, 9, 10 in figure 73 and 11, 12, 13, 14, 15, in figure 74 are all used for actual painting. The characteristics of these knives are as follows: No. 8 has a blade 5 inches long with a width at the tip of ½ inch (used for painting large surfaces with vigorous strokes). No. 9 has a blade 3¼ inches long; width at the tip, ⅛ inch.

Above: Fig. 64. Illustration showing the relative consistency of paint mixed with stand oil (left), linseed oil (center), and Copal Painting Medium. Right: Fig. 65. A rough canvas grain (top part of illustration) and grain covered with white lead paint by means of a palette knife (bottom part of illustration).

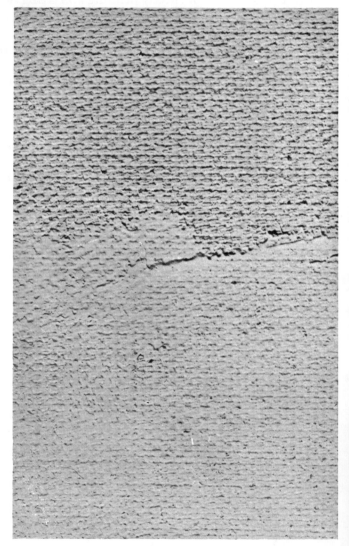

Fig. 66. Top left: A stippled impasto. Top right: The same impasto treated with a soft-hair blender. Bottom left: Paint texture produced by means of a bristle brush with "short" paint. Bottom right: Paint applied on top with a palette knife.

Top: Fig. 67A. A glaze applied to a hand-prepared canvas. Bottom: Fig. 67B. The same glaze covering a commercially prepared canvas.

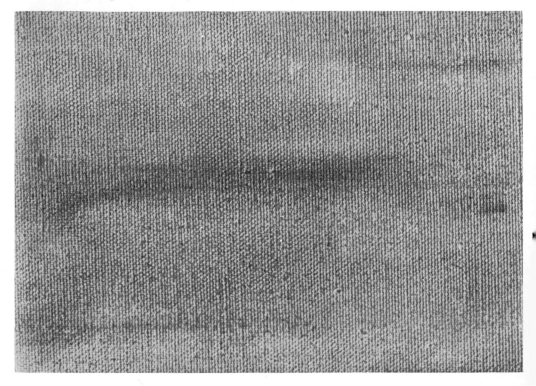

Upper: Fig. 68A. A scumble applied to a surface moistened with the painting medium. Lower: Fig. 68B. A scumble applied into a wet layer of paint.

Fig. 69. Top row: Effects produced with "short" paint.
Middle and bottom rows: Effects produced with long
paint.

Fig. 70. Brush with toed-in bristles, ordinary brush, and fuzzy sable brushes.

Fig. 71. Three sable brushes and soft-hair blender, at extreme right.

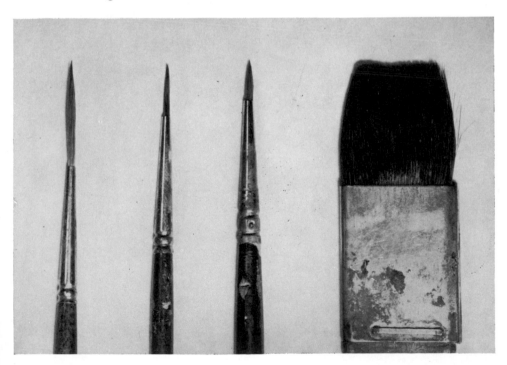

Fig. 72. Palette knives, left to right, numbers 1 to 5.

Fig. 73. Palette knives, left to right, numbers 6 to 10.

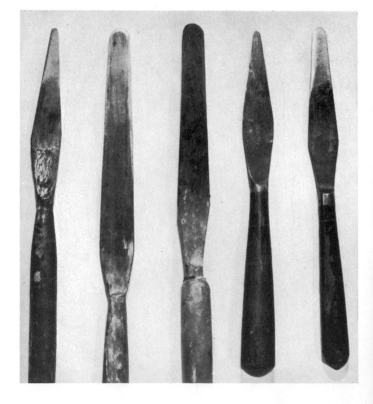

Fig. 74. Palette knives, left to right, numbers 11 to 15.

No. 10 is like the former, but its tip is $\frac{1}{4}$ inch wide. Both knives are quite flexible. The one with the narrower point is especially adapted for painting details, and so is knife No. 11, but its blade is rather stiff. This scalpel-like instrument is extremely efficient for painting over rough (dry) impasto. The next knives, Nos. 12, 13, and 14, are of great flexibility. Knives No. 12 and 15, for example, can, without any appreciable pressure, be brought into contact with the canvas for $2\frac{1}{2}$ inches. Such knives are well adapted to the delicate blending of colors, and the same applies to knife No. 8, which serves for blending large surfaces. Four inches of this blade can be brought into contact with the canvas with the greatest ease.

The Conditioning of Palette Knives

Most painters have undoubtedly found that it is quite difficult to obtain a knife that possesses the required properties for underpainting and painting. Most of the instruments seem to be designed by manufacturers who know nothing of the painter's requirements. These knives are more or less useless. The trowel-shaped knife and the one with a too rigid blade can be used for only one purpose—to scrape paint off the palette.

From the collection of fifteen knives reproduced here, only six were bought in a condition which permitted the performance of their appointed task. All the rest had to be improved in one way or another.

Assuming that the steel used in the manufacture of the knives is of good quality, a stiff knife can be made more elastic by taking off some of its thickness on a grinding wheel, for it is usually the thickness of the blade that makes it too stiff. (Motor-driven, high-speed wheels should not be used for this because they "burn" the steel blade.)

A standard knife blade is rigid at the handle, but from about the middle it should be much more elastic. Now let us assume that the blade is 4 inches long and half of it is fairly stiff. In this case, for all practical purposes only 1 inch of the blade will be in contact with the canvas when normal pressure is applied to the knife. However, if we thin the blade over its entire length, a 3-inch working surface can be gained. Such a quality of blade is most suitable for blending colors on the canvas.

Should a proper knife be unobtainable, instruments of any desired shape can be cut from the ordinary spatula which is available in stores carrying chemical equipment.

To change the thickness of a blade all that is needed is a grinding wheel. For altering the knife's shape, the knife will have to be cut on a steel-cutter in a tinsmith or machine shop. Whether ground down or cut, the edge of every blade will have to be treated with emery paper to remove its burr.

It should also be noted that any imperfections in a blade—nicks, dents, or other flaws—render the instrument useless. When cutting the knife, special care should be taken to round off the tip well so that no point remains on it which might mar the paint surface.

A steel knife, even if used only occasionally, will not rust, for the traces of oil left after wiping it clean protect it. I do not favor stainless steel knives, except for blending colors. It seems to me that their slick surface does not hold the paint well enough.

22

ANALYSIS OF PAINT TECHNIQUES

To ILLUSTRATE some of the technical problems discussed in the foregoing pages and in addition to the analyses of the centuries-old paintings discussed earlier, I have selected a few examples of my own work. This choice was made from the viewpoint of technique alone and not for any esthetic reasons. This is to say, the paintings reproduced on the following pages show clearly the characteristics that go into the making of a technique employing impasti of variable conformation, all kinds of delineations, calligraphy, glazes, and scumbles, as we see them imprinted by specific painter's tools. Naturally I can be absolutely sure of knowing which tools, paints, and so forth I myself employed.

Although all these characteristics are clearly manifest in the work of the old masters, as can be realized from the photographs shown in the first part of the book, I felt that contemporary painting differs from the older art, even though it uses the same physical means. It is my hope that these few illustrations may contribute something in the over-all understanding of the problems of paint manipulation.

"Danae" (9 by 12 inches), Detail, Figure 75

This photo, taken under raking light (that is, light held at such a slant as to make the texture stand out plastically), shows strong impasti on top of a thin underpainting which does not conceal the character of the canvas weave. The toned ground of the canvas carries an imprimatura of burnt sienna which remains visible here and there. Small, round, sable brushes were used on the areas of the detail and a palette knife on the sky (to the right). The white paint imparted its extra-long quality to the other colors mixed with it.

"Wilderness" (15 by 25 inches), Figures 76A, and 76B

Every imaginable technical device has been applied in this canvas. Let us consider figure 76A, which shows the right lower corner of the picture. In the underpainting, the strong impasto of the tree trunk was made with a stiff bristle brush which left its mark (long vertical strokes) in the body of the paint (white lead and umber). Over this (dry) underpainting, color (mars black and white) was applied with a palette knife. The very cool, gray tone received a final glaze of indian yellow to bring it into harmony in the general color scheme of the painting. I used genuine indian yellow here, a color which has been off the market now for more than a century. The pigment was ground in stand oil and thinned with Copal Painting Medium. That such a thin glaze, rubbed with the hand into the dry surface and possessing practically no body of its own, is vulnerable if subjected to the action of a strong organic solvent is understandable. In the restoration of paintings, these glazes are the first to disappear along with the dirt on top of them. The restorer, no matter how skillful, can have no inkling that the modification of the color with a yellow glaze was intentional and was not caused by a yellowed varnish film or surface scum. It can be assumed that such overcleaning must have been done on some of the old masters' paintings.

On the small area represented on this detail, which measures in the original 7 by 9 inches, a sable brush, bristle brush, and palette knife were used. Except for the tree trunk and the plants in the lower background, the paint is fairly smooth and semi-opaque. In some parts of the thicket it is so thin as to amount to a glaze.

In figure 76B, which shows verdant growth on top of a dead tree, the green paint is extra long. It was prepared from white lead, black, and cadmium yellow. All colors received admixtures of Copal Concentrate; the ivory black used, moreover, was partially freed of its original vehicle and ground in stand oil. The light, plastically raised accents of the foliage were painted rapidly into a dark (wet) green color of moderate thickness.

"Stone Bridge" (14 by 22 inches), Figures 77 and 77A

Three distinct treatments are evident in the detail (figure 77A). In the part of the rock to the right, opaque paint was applied with very few (perhaps three) strokes of the palette knife. The distant mountain view was scumbled on a rather rough, ocher underpainting that had been covered with a burnt sienna imprimatura. The scumble, in contrasting, bluish-gray color, permits the warm undertone to assert itself in small areas. For the calligraphic definition of the forest, zinc yellow was used. This color very easily becomes long with the addition of polymerized oil and thus lends itself to the finest plastic delineations. The shaded part of the rock to the left was underpainted in pink and carries a glaze of umber and prussian blue.

"St. Christopher" (30 by 36 inches), Figure 78

With the exception of the delineations (that is, the contouring of the details) and the scumbles of the sky (put into a wet, viscous, dark paint), the entire painting was executed with a variety of palette knives. Here one may see the importance of using differently shaped knives, not only to facilitate intricate operations but to produce different textures and thus avoid that monotony of surface which the use of a single palette knife often spreads throughout the entire picture. Some parts of the rock show large forms; but some small facets are painted on several underpaintings of appreciable impasto. Here a special knife (see figure 74 [knife No. 11]) proved to be most efficient. Only such a pointed, scalpel-like, rather stiff instrument can move over the rough impasti underpaintings with the requisite force and efficiency. Its pointed blade is also capable of modeling even small details with precision.

In painting the water, over a gray-bluish underpainting (of white, umber, and prussian blue), a darker glaze of the same color mixtures was applied. White color was scumbled into this glaze while wet by means of a rather stiff knife. Practically the entire river area, with the exception of a very few brushstrokes which can be seen here and there, was painted with the knife. Skillful handling of an appropriate palette knife will produce either straight or curved lines as fine as desired.

"Tower of Babel" (28 by 44 inches), Figures 79 and 79A.

The maxim held by the old masters that a proper underpainting constitutes half the work on a painting should perhaps be qualified by adding: except when the underpainting amounts to three-quarters or more of the total work. The latter is certainly true in the case of the "Tower of Babel."

It can be seen from the detail in figure 79*A*, which shows a part of the Tower and the fields beyond it, that the impasto of the several underpaintings is quite heavy. That these impasti were well blended, as can be seen by the brush strokes, facilitated the final painting and permitted the separation of the object from the background to be achieved in a manner suitable to the medium.

It may be of interest to note that, in the underpainting of the tower, the parts which are light in the final painting appeared darker than the areas which would eventually be shown in shade. The explanation is that areas of shadow were first underpainted in a light color, in order to be treated with glazes. The impasti of the final painting are all gathered in the areas of light.

The shadow cast on the fields by the Tower was not considered in the underpainting. The sunlit landscape was painted first, and the area where the shadow was to be cast was kept free of impasto. This shadow was glazed as soon as the paint had solidified, which took about two days. A glaze applied on such a fresh paint film has the best chance of surviving, for it incorporates itself with the paint proper and thus becomes an integral part of the solid stratum.

"Rock" (14 by 16 inches), Detail, Figure 80

This photograph of a detail also reveals heavy impasto, but whereas the underpainting of the "Tower" was built up with the brush, the "Rock" was first "stippled" with a palette knife. Upon this (dry) impasto the final painting was done, also with the knife. The details were engraved, as it were, onto the stiff (wet) paint with fine sable brushes in thin, liquid paint. In contrast to the rock area, the foreground carries only one underpainting, which is covered with thin paint applied with but a few strokes of the knife. Here the texture of the canvas remains plainly visible.

"Painter" (10 by 12 inches), Detail, Figure 81

The importance of having a hand-prepared priming when painting thinly is apparent in this composition. It is obvious that, if the texture of the fabric looked like that shown in figure 67*B*, much of the sensuous feeling that we get from the present conformation of the paint texture would be lost, and the mechanical character of the surface would seriously impair the paint quality and hence the general effect of the work. In the area of the canvas directly before the painter as he faces the easel, the original underpainting was left uncovered. The texture of the part of the canvas that depicts the floor is also visible, through the glaze of burnt sienna which is laid on evenly in applications now denser, now thinner.

A characteristic example of treatment in open color can be seen on the foot of the figure in front, which has been merely outlined against the background (the floor). Such marginal treatment of details adds a certain airiness to the whole by preventing any one detail from becoming too important.

"Island" (30 by 35 inches), Figure 82

In the sea surrounding the Island, the texture of the canvas is distinctly revealed. Here the very sturdy fabric, showing threads of irregular thickness, received three layers of white-lead priming, two layers of underpainting, and one final overpainting. In spite of these six coats of paint, the canvas still shows its heavy texture, and this can be attributed to the direction in which the palette knife was moved. Depending on the direction of the knife's motion—that is, whether its stroke is going with the woof or the warp or diagonally to them—the grain of the fabric changes in appearance.

As variegated in texture as this area (the sea) appears, if it were to prevail throughout the whole picture it would become disturbing simply because an extraneous element, the texture of the canvas, would gain undue dominance. Therefore, the entire right side of the island (the one in shade) was underpainted in such a manner as to make the character of the support almost disappear. Here glazes of various degrees of density make up the entire painting. Let me repeat that the longevity of such glazes depends not only on the nature of the medium used, but also on the timing of its application, for the glaze and the paint underlying it should dry out to one solid film.

"St. John" (16 by 18 inches), Detail, Figure 83

The head, underpainted several times, does not show any appreciable impasto, for the paint layers were all smoothed out with a knife. The background is treated on the whole as an open color. This color extends beyond the delineated motifs; it is not arrested by the motifs' boundaries. The background (underpainted in a yellowish

233

color) is glazed with burnt sienna and variegated with light scumbles (mostly on the upper part) and in places by darker, denser glazes, particularly at the bottom. The whole procedure is simplified, inasmuch as drawing with paint supplements actual painting. Here the character of the calligraphy accounts for the ultimate effect.

When you use an open color, economy in the number of colors used is of great importance; the more restricted the palette, the more agreeable the effects. In the painting under discussion, the following colors were used: naples yellow, ocher, burnt sienna, black, and white. In the underpainting, the background was executed with ocher, some cadmium yellow, and white; and the head was painted several times in grisaille prepared from prussian blue, ocher, umber, and white.

"Tree" (20 by 40 inches), Figures 84 and 84A

A treatment related to the open color method is seen in the foliage of the tree, which seems to explode into the sky. There are, in practice, three ways of treating the confluence of one painted surface with another. First, the surfaces can meet at a sharply defined contour. Let us consider the foliage, for example. The leaves can be painted on top of a dry sky, thus producing hard, unyielding edges. Second, blending in various degrees of softness can be attempted; that is, the outer edge can be made fuzzy or blurred by various means, such as brushing both (wet) surfaces, the sky and the foliage, together with a bristle or sable brush or a soft-hair blender.

For this to be done successfully with a bristle brush, the paint should be of considerable viscosity. A sable brush used in any kind of paint produces soft, delicate transitions, and a still greater degree of blending can be achieved by means of a soft-hair blender. Then again, blending can be effected by "dragging" a brush containing very little paint over the *dry* adjoining area. The brush encounters only the protruding grain of the fabric (or the texture of paint), and will, therefore, produce a blurred contour.

The third way of meeting the problem of contour was used in painting the foliage of the "Tree" (see figure 84A). Here all the blending was done in the underpainting. Thus the underpainting of the foliage and the sky proceeded as follows: the foliage, in this instance the prongs of the branches, was underpainted in yellow and the sky in a light blue. The blending was done with the knife by moving it rapidly from the yellow area into the blue, and then vice versa, thus merging the opposing colors. Of course, both colors must be wet in this procedure but must not be applied with appreciable impasto, for a thick color would impede the creation of delicate tran-

234

sitions. This, then, is the underpainting to use in painting final contours. Whether painting or merely delineating, as the case may be, the color proper of the foliage (the yellow) goes beyond its assigned area into this blended area in its confluence with the sky. Thus the foliage does not terminate with its own contour, but it reverberates beyond it, as it were, in overtones.

This kind of effect is, *de facto,* a modification of an open color. However, in its over-all aspect it is pictorial in nature rather than draftsmanlike.

On the basis of the existing data of research and our empirical knowledge, I have endeavored to communicate to the serious student of paint technology all that seems to me to be important in the process of a proper picture build-up.

I hope that this book will contribute toward a better understanding of the ways and means followed by the old masters, in the belief that these ways and means can still best serve the contemporary painter in realizing his own pictorial aims.

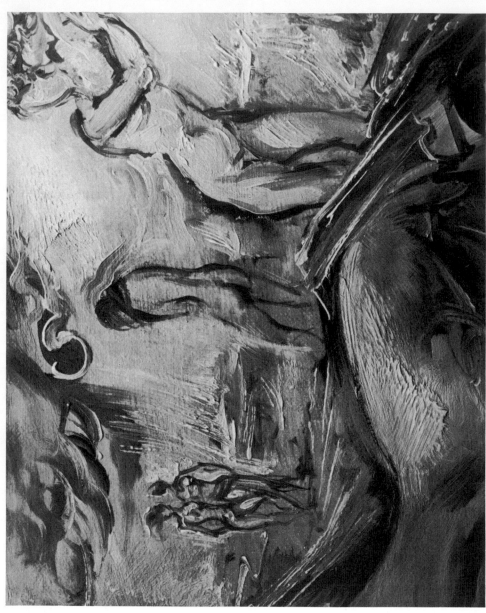

Fig. 75. "Da-naë" (detail).

Fig. 76A

Fig. 76B

Fig. 76

*"Wilderness." Above:
the complete picture.
Right, top and bottom:
two details.*

"The Stone Bridge."
Right: The complete
painting. Below: Detail
of central part.

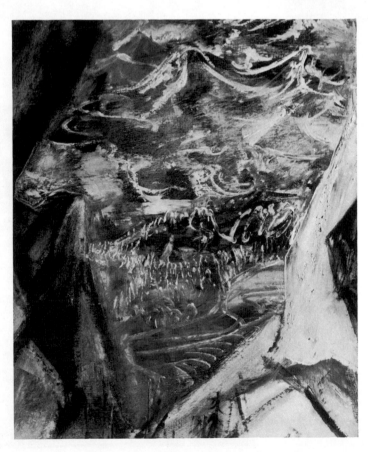

Fig. 77A

Above: Fig. 78. "St. Christopher."

Right: Fig. 79. "The Tower of Babel."

*Above: Fig. 79A. De-
tail from "The Tow-
er of Babel." Right:
Fig. 80. "The Rock"
(detail).*

Fig. 81. "The Painter" (detail).

Fig. 82. "The Island."

(Associated American Artists
Galleries)

Fig. 83. "St. John" (detail).

Above: Fig. 84. "The Tree."
Right: Fig. 84A. Detail from the
upper right area of the same
painting.

GLOSSARY

Aerial perspective. Perspective relying on diminishing color intensity to show increased distance.

Alla prima. Aiming from the start at the final effect while painting wet-in-wet.

Balsam. Exudate from certain kinds of coniferous trees.

Binder. The medium that binds or unites the pigment particles.

Chiaroscuro. A clear division between light and shade.

Conformation of paint. The structure of dried paint.

Filler. Inert pigment generally added to paints as an adulterant.

Gel. A jellylike substance.

Gesso. Italian for chalk; designates a priming prepared from size and a white pigment such as whiting.

Glaze. A transparent film of a darker color applied to a light underpainting.

Grisaille. Underpainting in gray color.

Gum (turpentine, damar, arabic). Exudates from certain trees (sometimes unspecifically applied to resins).

Hiding power. The degree of opacity in paint.

Hygroscopic. Having the tendency to absorb water.

Impasto. Painting applied in plastic relief.

Imprimatura. A glaze applied to a canvas before painting, and thinned with a varnish (not oil) medium.

Linoxyn. A dried linseed-oil film.

Long paint. Paint which is stringy and which when applied to a surface, has the tendency to seek the level (that is, does not retain its original conformation exactly). Such paint is always soft-edged.

Paint. Pigment compounded in oil.

Pastose. Painted thickly.

Pigment. Dry color, without the binder.

Painterly. Relying on tonal rather than lineal effects.

Priming. A surface applied to a support preliminary to painting.

Polymerization. Changes in molecular grouping of certain liquids.

Relining. Mounting an old canvas to a new one.

Resin, hard. Preserved exudates from coniferous trees now extinct.

Resin, soft. Exudates from living coniferous trees.

Running. Thermal processing of hard resin.

Scumble. A semi-opaque application of a light color on a darker under-painting.

Short paint. Paint which retains a sharp configuration when applied with the brush or knife.

Siccative (dryer). Metallic salts used for speeding up the drying of paint.

Size. An aqueous solution of glue.

Stabilizers. Materials used to keep the pigment suspended in oil.

Stand oil. Linseed oil cooked at high temperatures in the absence of air.

Stringy paint. See long paint.

Support. Surface used when painting.

Tempera. An emulsion of aqueous and oily liquids.

Tooth. Roughness or graininess of a surface.

Varnish. A solution of resin in a diluent.

Venice turpentine. A soft semiliquid resin obtained from a certain kind of larch tree.

Vehicle. A binder for pigments.

Viscosity. Relative stickiness of a liquid. The higher viscosity, the slower the flow.

INDEX OF TECHNIQUES

deficiency of, 139; synthetic, 206; finish, wax, 205
retouching with varnish, 203

saponin, 199, 209
scumble, 91, 99, 168, 169
siccative: cobalt, 192; colors, 192-193
stabilizers, 171-174; green earth as, 172-173
stand oil, 8, 12, 65, 137
stand-oil paint, 134

tempera, 3, 7, 23, 35; egg-yolk, 7; gum, 8, 21
trickling, 203
tube paint, 133-134

tubes, filling of, 183
turpentine, 14, 136

umber, 192, 213
underpainting, 156-159; tools for, 160

varnish: Copal Varnish, 200; Copal Painting Medium (as varnish), 202-203; damar, 202, 203; for imprimatura, 201; retouching with, 203
varnishing paintings, 201-202

wax, carnauba, 204-205
wax-resin finish, 205
white lead for priming, 201

xylene, 199